INTERVIEW FOR A TEACHING JOB 2022-3

*The definitive guide to interviews for a job as a teacher, **HoD**, **HoY**, **AHT**, **DHT** or headteacher*

THEO GRIFF

DISCLAIMER: This book has been written with reasonable skill and care, and in good faith as the personal opinion of the author. However, it gives advice or suggestions on a provisional basis that readers are free to accept or reject, using their own personal and professional judgment, with no liability being incurred by the author.

This book relates to teaching posts in England and Wales, mainly in schools but also in colleges, although many points will also be relevant elsewhere.

REVISED AND UPDATED FOR THE SCHOOL YEAR 2022-3

TABLE OF CONTENTS

5. Other activities as part of the selection process

The observed lesson

Visit round the school

Student panel

Meeting colleagues

Written task

Withdrawing before the interview

6. The interview panel

The aims of the interview for the panel

Some things that you probably do not know about the interview panel

How to cope with inappropriate questions

The panel is probably inexperienced, untrained and nervous

7. The interview – general overview

8. The 5 mistakes that teachers make in an interview

The five mistakes to avoid in an interview

9. The wrong first impression

10. The wrong self-presentation

What to wear to the interview

Do the smell test

Horrid personal habits

Body language

Facial expression

11. The wrong sort of talking

Talking too fast

22. Senior Leadership interviews

Your impact at the interview as a prospective school leader

23. Preparation for the SLT interview

Information available

The qualities sought

Mind mapping

24. The SLT selection process

Activities for SLT selection days

General overview of the different activities in a SLT interview

In-tray exercises

The carousel of activities

The student council

The presentation

Why you were asked not to come to the second stage interview

25. The aftermath

INTRODUCTION

After more than 20 years in education leadership, and over a decade of supporting both teachers and headteachers on an online education advice forum, Theo Griff has written this book full of up-to-date tips and suggestions to help you nail that job as a teacher, a middle or a senior leader, through an effective interview.

This book incidentally can also act as a guide to best practice in interviewing for new or inexperienced interviewers, a newly-appointed head of department, perhaps, or a governor and other interview panel members in a small school that does not often appoint new colleagues.

Interview for a Teaching Job 2022-3 provides clear advice on many issues that you may be wondering about, and perhaps even some that you have never thought of, given from the perspective of both the interviewee and the interviewer. It is a companion volume to *Applying for a Teaching Job 2022-3*, also available in Kindle format and paperback.

REVISED AND UPDATED FOR THE SCHOOL YEAR 2022-3

SCHOOL LEADERS COMMENT ON THIS BOOK

Headteacher of large secondary school: *Clearly written and comprehensive, this is a treasure chest of advice, tips and insider information for the candidates. The perspective of an experienced interviewer is invaluable for novice interviewers too.*

Consultant, Ambition School Leadership (formerly Future Leaders): *I'd make this book compulsory reading for all PGCE students - and for the NPQH, for that matter. I work with senior leadership candidates and it would make my life so much easier if they all read and used the advice here.*

Vice-Principal, Sixth Form College: *I was surprised by how much I learned, and how much I enjoyed reading this book, since I thought I was pretty experienced in interviewing, and knew a lot about it already.*

Secondary headteacher in the North: *Theo, it's fabulous! I really, really enjoyed reading it, which is remarkable and to your credit, given how familiar I am with the topic.*

REVIEWS OF EARLIER VERSIONS

I never expected to find a book on interviews so useful. Having in the past looked at generic interview books many times in previous years I thought it might be more of the same vagueness, but this book is a real gem, written especially for teachers preparing for an interview. Theo gives excellent advice which helps your thinking so you can tailor what you might say in an interview, so it is right for you.

I would highly recommend this text for its step-by-step guidance on how to nail the teaching interview process. It's comprehensive and accessible for everyone, from those just starting out to those attempting the loftier heights of SLT. It also comes with little snippets of anecdote regarding interviewer and interviewee faux pas that are invaluable and also add a smattering of humour to what could otherwise be a stressful experience. The virtual / online interview section is particularly useful in these current circumstances where interviewing in person simply isn't feasible. An essential read all round.

The book was INVALUABLE. Even down to tiny details of how to physically present yourself and how to answer tricky questions. At the end of my interview day I came away feeling incredibly happy with the way I had performed and knowing that I could not have done anything better. I also felt so much better about the specific way I had answered many of the questions posed to me, answers that I might have given quite differently prior to reading the book. Ultimately, I got the job, on a unanimous vote of confidence from the whole panel apparently. Thank you so much Theo!

Yet another fantastic book written by Theo Griff. Having read 'Applying for a teaching job', with interest, I was eager to read 'Interview for a teaching job'. I absolutely hate interviews, and never really feel prepared no matter what I do. However, this book is packed with a wealth of really useful information, providing the reader with lots of helpful, practical tips and strategies so you can be more fully prepared and confident during interviews.

I am an experienced teacher but when facing my first interview for a few years I downloaded Theo's book to aid my preparation. It is concise, funny and so helpful. The section on remote interviews was particularly useful as the circumstances surrounding my interview changed and it was eventually conducted via Zoom. If you are new to the profession or experienced, you will definitely benefit from the advice offered in this book - buy it! Thank you, Theo, for writing this superb book.

If you're applying for a school teaching job - or you're involved in interviewing candidates for teaching posts - this is a book you should definitely read. Valuable advice from an experienced education professional will guide you through the whole process.

Really succinct and helpful guidance about interviewing for teaching posts in the UK. Any prospective candidates would do well to give this a read and most interviewers should also!

1. BEFORE YOU START

WHERE NOT TO LOOK FOR INTERVIEW ADVICE AND OBSERVED LESSON IDEAS

T here is a lot of advice available on interviews: from Careers Guidance departments at universities for students applying for their first job, advice in books, and above all, advice on the internet.

Beware!

A great deal of it is totally inappropriate for interviews for teaching jobs in England and Wales. One website suggests, for example, that you should take to the interview a thank-you card to leave at Reception on the way out; another that the moment that you leave the building after your interview, you should whip out your phone to thank them for interviewing you. This, we are told, will enable you to leave a strong final impression.

The strong final impression that these tactics would leave in most schools is that you are unaware of what is and what is not an appropriate way to act in a school context. There's the matter of good manners and politeness, which is absolutely appropriate and necessary in an interview situation, and then there's pure and simple obsequiousness, which those 'tips' above most definitely are.

So where should you get the answers to the questions that are posed at interview? The answer is simple: from yourself. You are the one who will be doing the job; getting answers from elsewhere is not showing that you could be either effective or happy in a post. Getting appointed on the basis of someone else's ideas is setting yourself up for potential failure, distress and unhappiness. In the section on preparing for the interview, this book will show you how to develop your own answers based on your own strengths and experience.

Reading books or website with titles such as *Answers to tough interview questions* is, quite frankly, to be avoided. Most of these are US-focussed and business-orientated, so not the sort of answer that would be appreciated when you are interviewing for a KS2 class teacher post. And sometimes they are so hackneyed as to be unbelievable. Here is a perfect example of this, in a model answer given in reply to a query about why someone is not currently employed; imagine this answer being given by a teacher you know claiming to have left the security of a full-time post for supply.

I'm looking for a bigger challenge and to grow my career, but didn't feel like I could give equal attention both to my job search and to my full-time work responsibilities. It didn't seem ethical to slack off from my former job in order to conduct my job search, and so I left the company.

No, I am not going to believe that!

School-orientated sources are sometimes not any better. Here is some advice about lesson planning from one of them that purports to show you how to master the teacher interview:

Lesson planning is important in that it prevents you from

running out of activities halfway through the lesson. No teacher wants to be caught with nothing to teach. (...) Games such as Hangman are a really useful way of filling in extra time and are a great way of imparting useful knowledge and interacting with students.

No comment needed here, I believe, except that Ofsted might not quite be of the same opinion.

However, there is another danger with sources of this kind, even - or perhaps I should say especially – if they are school-orientated. The danger is that the model answer that you found in a book or website, and gave so confidently in your interview, has also been seen by other candidates, or indeed by the interviewing panel themselves. Your answer may thus have a follow-up question: *Can you explain why your answer is virtually identical to the answer given by a previous candidate?* Or alternatively: *Last night I read a book called 'Interview questions and answers for teachers'. I wonder if you have read it too, because your last two answers seem to have come straight from this book.*

For this reason, I am warning you now that this book does not contain a long list of questions with their model answers. A question seen regularly on TES Community, a recently-closed popular online education advice forum was *"I've got an interview for the post of X next week; can anyone give me a list of the questions that I might be asked, with the answers, please?"* This query tended to be met with a polite refusal and the reasons why, often resulting in an outraged reply from the first poster *"I thought this was meant to be a help forum!"* Despite this, people continued to ask for these answers to be supplied; we even saw it come from prospective headteachers, which didn't tend to fill one with confidence about their ability to do the job.

I have seen, on Amazon, reviews of other teacher interview books which say: *There was* (sic) *no answers in the book which disappointed me.* In a similar vein, another reviewer writes: *It didn't have sample answers, just questions so I was disappointed as I was looking for a book which had answers too*. Candidates for a post who cannot devise their own answers to interview questions (yet alone who communicate so ungrammatically) would be quickly unmasked at interview by experienced interviewers, I'm afraid, and this book will not provide you with that false support. There are occasional examples of a question with a poor and an improved answer, to illustrate a technique, but no page after page of what should be the answer to 100 different questions.

Stop reading now if that is what you are hoping for.

Internet sources for teaching ideas, plans and resources for your observed lesson are also a no-no; not even the excellent TES Resources, unless it is your own resource, uploaded there by you. Even then I feel that it would be best to have something to which no other candidate has access. Using these internet sources can be a recipe for disaster, not success. I will explain why later on, in the section on preparing the observed lesson.

Finally, if you are an NQT, do be a little cautious in accepting blindly the advice of your university tutor, as they normally do not have experience of appointing teachers to positions in schools. They mean well, of course, but their experience is often well out of date, or they simply lack senior leadership experience in interviewing candidates for school posts. Your school-based mentor, however, is probably a head of department and does have this experience, so their advice is often very helpful.

So where should you get your advice? From this book, and from other people like me who have very many years of experience of appointing teachers to a wide range of educational establishments, have read thousands of application forms and supporting statements, and have conducted very many interviews. I personally have interviewed approximately 1,000 candidates for jobs at all levels in schools, colleges and universities, in the UK and in British schools abroad. My continuing role as a consultant for school appointments means that I still do interview candidates. I have enormous experience in what makes me, and other members of appointment panels, want to "buy" a particular candidate or say, "Thank you, but no". In reading this book, you are going to learn how to sell yourself to the interviewing panel.

I shall sometimes briefly repeat information at different points in the book so that you have all the right advice to hand when reading any particular section, and also reproduce short sections of my previous Amazon Kindle book *Applying for a Teaching Job 2022-3*, where you need the information again at this point.

2. SHORTLISTING

T he interview panel is the same group of people, usually, who do the shortlisting. A headteacher says: *In my school, it is part of our policy that only people who have been involved in shortlisting can be part of the interview panel.* This alone should give you confidence when going to interview, because they have already picked you out as impressive, they have decided that you are capable of doing the job, of making a valuable contribution to their school.

How many people are shortlisted? It depends on the school, and on the number of suitable applicants. I once shortlisted only two applicants from a very poor field – poor both numerically and in quality. Some schools have written or unwritten rules that they will never shortlist fewer than three or four candidates, so if there are insufficient suitable applicants, they re-advertise. I was happy that both these applicants were strong contenders from their applications, and was proved correct when we interviewed them, as they turned out to be two exceptional candidates. The decision was therefore taken to appoint them both, on the grounds that I didn't wish to lose either of them to another school, and that an extra maths teacher is always useful.

I have seen occasions where schools choose to interview eight candidates; I believe this to be too many, as it is too disruptive to the school (too many classes receiving observed lessons, too many staff involved in observing, too long for the panel to be out of circulation), and frankly, just too tiring and boring for the panel. I consider five or six to be the optimal number. But as in my example above where only two were invited, a school should not invite someone who does not seem suitable, just to make up the numbers.

So how does the panel shortlist you? Best practice is firstly to have blind shortlisting. This means that when an application is received in the office, a member of support staff is in charge of removing from the applications the front page, that is, the one with the personal details of the candidate. The application is given a number, and only then are the remaining pages photocopied and passed to the shortlisting panel. This means that selection is done blind, and not based on the personal identity of the candidates.

Not all schools do this, however and since the rise of academies and free schools, what was previously good practice transmitted out of local authorities may well have morphed into something quite different. Don't expect the kind of equal opportunities-orientated practice described above to be the norm everywhere, because some schools are doing their own thing. That is unfortunate for them, as it could leave them open to accusations of unlawful discrimination, without this as their defence.

The next procedure for shortlisting has traditionally been that a large table is drawn up with the criteria (taken from the job description and person specification) in the left-hand column, then a number of columns, one for each applicant, where a tick or cross is placed next to each criterion, finally putting a Y or a N at the very bottom of each column indicating a wish to invite them in for an interview. Here is an example of these tables.

EXAMPLE OF TABLE USED BY SCHOOLS TO SHORTLIST CANDIDATES

Criteria	Candidate 1	Candidate 2	Candidate 3
Qualified to teach and work in the UK	✓	✓	✓
Good Honours degree in main subject	✓	X	✓
Successful teaching to GCSE and A-level	✓	✓	GCSE only
Evidence of driving up standards of achievement for all	✓	?	✓
Effective behaviour management	?	?	✓
Commitment to regular ongoing professional development	✓	X	✓
Shortlist Y/N	Y	N	?

When I am managing an appointment procedure, the

shortlisting table has the following header:

We do blind shortlisting for all posts. In order for us to achieve our aim of equal opportunities for all candidates, please mark with a Y those boxes where you believe the candidate to comply with the different criteria for appointment, with a ? those where s/he partly complies, and an X for a distinct negative. This will allow you to identify those candidates to shortlist. Please use continuation sheets as necessary, amending the column heading numbers if there are more than 30 candidates. N.B. this sheet will be signed by you and kept in our Central Records as proof that the procedures have been carried out.

The last sentence is important; I was horrified to discover once that an additional criterion – M/F – had been added to the end of the sheet by one member of a shortlisting panel, who had gone carefully through the applications noting where candidates went to single-sex schools, or played rugby, had knitting as a hobby, or anything else which it was believed could perhaps indicate gender. This colleague felt that the gender balance in the staffroom could be impacted negatively by the new appointee.

Memo to headteachers: ensure that all staff, governors and trust members involved in appointments are aware of the legal issues surrounding appointment, especially the protected characteristics under the Equality Act 2010: age, disability, gender reassignment, marriage and civil partnership, pregnancy and maternity, race, religion or belief, gender, and sexual orientation.

CONTACTING CANDIDATES ABOUT THEIR APPLICATION

After sending off your application comes the nail-biting period, waiting to see if it has been successful in gaining you an interview. If you are fortunate, you may get an acknowledgement of receipt of your application, especially if the school has set up an automatic reply to their applications e-mail account. But nowadays it is very common to hear nothing after e-mailing off the application on which you spent so much time. It is also unusual nowadays even to receive a polite response informing you that you have not been selected for interview. So you just sit and bite your nails.

There used to be a time – when I was a bushy-tailed young teacher – when schools would write to you more than once during the applications process. You applied for a job (by post - there was no other way), and they wrote back to acknowledge receipt of the application. They then wrote again to inform you that your application was – or was not - being taken forward to the interview stage. However, they didn't write to tell you the result of the interview, because it was carried out differently back then.

In my early teaching days, the candidates all stayed after the interviews, sitting together in a room with nothing to do, until a secretary came into the room and said: *"Miss Brown, the panel would like to speak to you"*. Miss Brown then left, and the remainder of us waited until the door opened again with either the announcement: *"Miss Brown has accepted the post"*, or *"Mr Smith, the panel would like to speak to you"*. That meant that Miss Brown had turned it down. A daunting experience, sitting waiting in the company of the other candidates, and Mr Smith knew that he was only second choice. The rest of us knew that we were no choice at all, very fast.

Subsequently, of course, the disappointed candidates undertook the 'walk of shame' out of school. Someone I know, who was interviewed for a deputy headship in London in the early 90s and got through to the final interview with one other candidate, found herself doing the walk of shame down four flights of steps with the entire governing body panel. There were more than 20 of them.

Nowadays the procedure is that each candidate leaves at the end of their interview, having given contact telephones and times to a secretary, so that they can be phoned with the decision of the panel. More about this later.

In the past at least, unlike nowadays, you knew whether or not you were selected for interview. Many schools now warn you in their application information that they will not write back to you: *We shall be holding interviews in the week beginning 21 May. If you have not heard from us by then, you should assume that your application has not been successful.*

I tend to agree with those who find this a little discourteous. But on the other hand, a school receiving 60, 100 or even more applications just cannot afford the time for the secretary to look up all the e-mail addresses and inform the unsuccessful candidates, so I also tend to agree with them that it is not practical.

REQUESTING REFERENCES

S o you sent off your application, seemingly into a black hole, then when one of your referees tells you that s/he has received a request for a reference, you become very hopeful at this sign of life from the school to which you applied, expecting to be called to interview. And in most cases, rightly so, although not always, as I explain later.

Usually, the request for a reference drops into your headteacher's in-box within an hour of the invitation to interview dropping into yours. The headteacher will probably see it before you do, as you are probably teaching and thus less likely to be checking the e-mail on your phone or computer. I hope that you followed the advice in **Applying for a Teaching Job 2022-3** and talked to the headteacher about this application, asking his/her permission to be named as a referee, so that the reference request does not come as a surprise.

The statutory guidance to schools is that they should always obtain references before interview. Here is the relevant extract from **Keeping children safe in education 2022 Statutory guidance for schools and colleges, 1 September 2022.**

Employment history and references.

The purpose of seeking references is to allow employers to obtain factual information to support appointment decisions.

Schools and colleges should obtain references before interview, where possible, this allows any concerns raised to be explored further with the referee and taken up with the candidate at interview.

Schools and colleges should:

• not accept open references e.g. to whom it may concern

• not rely on applicants to obtain their reference

• ensure any references are from the candidate's current employer and have been completed by a senior person with appropriate authority (if the referee is school or college based, the reference should be confirmed by the headteacher/ principal as accurate in respect of any disciplinary investigations)

• obtain verification of the individual's most recent relevant period of employment where the applicant is not currently employed

• secure a reference from the relevant employer from the last time the applicant worked with children (if not currently working with children), if the applicant has never worked with children, then ensure a reference from their current employer

• always verify any information with the person who provided the reference

• ensure electronic references originate from a legitimate source

• contact referees to clarify content where information is vague or insufficient information is provided

• compare the information on the application form with that in the reference and take up any discrepancies with the candidate

• establish the reason for the candidate leaving their current or most recent post, and,

• ensure any concerns are resolved satisfactorily before appointment is confirmed.

COMMON MISCONCEPTIONS ABOUT REFERENCES

I have met teachers who believe that a headteacher – or anyone else – cannot write a poor or negative reference for a teacher. Goodness knows where they get that idea from, as it certainly is not true. A referee has every right to write a negative reference about a colleague who is not carrying out duties to the required standard or is in breach of any part of the *Teachers' Standards.*

Why, indeed, should a referee be legally obliged to give Bluebeard or Jack the Ripper a glowing reference if they were poor teachers and a danger to children in addition? It just would not make sense. References are to enable schools to appoint someone who will be an excellent teacher, make an overall positive contribution to the school community, and who will not represent a danger to children, staff or visitors to the school. So references can be negative, and should be if necessary. There would otherwise be no point in having them, as they are supposed to be an objective statement of the strengths and weaknesses of a candidate. It thus follows that if there are more weaknesses than strengths, then the reference will be negative.

However, any reference, whether it be a positive or a negative one, should always be totally factual and firmly based on evidence, not on someone's likes, dislikes or prejudices. A reference should thus always be objective and evidence-based, not subjective and based on gossip. I would consider a "poor" reference to be one that was inaccurate and full of unsubstantiated subjective views, rather than one that was truthful, balanced and objective. Therefore, the headteacher or other referee **is** allowed to include negative but substantiated points such as:

Ms X wasn't a good teacher (and give examples of observations that support this view)

Mr Y was often late or absent (and say that the attendance evidence shows this)

Mrs W's behaviour management was poor (records of observations show this)

Parents complained about Dr Z's treatment of students (records show this)

The legal requirement is for a reference to be fair and factually accurate. If, because of negligent misstatement (inclusion of inaccurate or omission of important information), you suffer detriment (loss), then you may claim damages. As a result, most headteachers, heads of department and other referees are very careful to be totally factual and balanced in their references. There will doubtless occasionally be the exception, but in general they are extremely careful, as they do not wish either the colleague or the new school to challenge them for something that is not quite right.

Another misconception is that your headteacher is obliged to give you a reference. In fact, no employer is obliged to write a reference, unless it says so in your contract or other legal agreement. One exception could be if you have a settlement agreement that says that a specific agreed reference will be given. In these cases, the Head is indeed obliged to respond to reference requests as set out in the agreement.

Generally, however, despite there being no obligation to do so, headteachers do write references for colleagues, but it is courteous to go and see the head at an early stage in the application process to request permission to put them down as a referee.

Something else that may come as a surprise to many teachers is that a school to whom they apply is not limited to contacting only those people who have been given as referees. You have given your current headteacher (as required) and a head of department from six years ago, but nobody from the school in between where you were only employed for two terms. There may be nothing suspicious at all about that short stay (although it would have made sense to explain it away in just one short sentence in your application), but a school can ring them up and ask if there was a problem, even though there is nobody from there as a referee in your application.

As we clarified above, the law says that if a reference is written, the employer has a duty to ensure that it is fair and factually accurate. However, if you suspect that something inaccurate has been said, you are in a difficult position, because contrary to further common belief, you do not have a right to be shown your reference by your referee. Neither the **Freedom of Information Act** nor the **Data Protection Act** says that the headteacher must show you what s/he has written in response to a reference request.

I could write – and have written in the past – half a dozen pages on this. But I'll just sum up and say: try asking your headteacher anyway to show you what was sent in support of your application. Many schools and local authorities have an "*Open References*" policy, where what is written about you is open for you to see. So ask, and you may well get to see it. If your headteacher is unwilling to show you the reference, you could try asking the school to whom it was sent. You might well get lucky, and they send it to you in full, not redacted, (because they haven't read or understood the regulations). But do not believe those who assure you that you have an absolute right to see your reference.

LONGLISTING AND SHORTLISTING

Some schools carry out a longlisting procedure before shortlisting the five or six candidates who will come to interview. This means that instead of selecting the actual candidates for interview, they select a dozen or more, write to the referees of these longlisted candidates, and will then proceed to shortlist from this longer list.

Why do they do this? It may be just because they want to have more information about candidates to help them come to a decision. Another reason may be that they want to make sure that they have the possibility of calling in another suitable candidate at short notice if they receive an unsatisfactory reference from someone they had provisionally earmarked for interview, or if a shortlisted candidate withdraws before the interview. Having a pool of already-referenced-candidates makes life easier when they are working to a deadline.

So what is the procedure for shortlisting from the longlisted candidates?

When they have received all the references, they then look again at the whole set of information for each applicant: application form, letter or supporting statement and executive summary, and references. I would like to emphasise that they consider the whole package again for each candidate, not just the references. And having considered again all the information, then they whittle them down to five or six.

I emphasise the fact that they look at the whole of the information because often applicants who hear that references have been called for, yet they do not get called to interview, are tempted to blame their references for not being glowing enough. That is not necessarily so. Your references may be quite outstanding, but the panel may decide that another candidate just has more overall to offer the school, and so on this occasion you are not shortlisted.

This longlisting can be used for all levels of post, from classroom teachers to headteachers.

So does calling for a reference mean that you've been shortlisted for interview? Usually, but not always, is the answer.

WHEN WILL YOU HEAR THAT YOU'VE BEEN SHORTLISTED FOR INTERVIEW?

I wish I could tell you that, but I am afraid that I can't, as there is just no set rule. Some schools will sit down on the morning of the closing date and have shortlisting sorted in time to send out the invitations to interview that very afternoon. Some may even invite very promising candidates before the closing date, because they are convinced that they are what they want, and add extra invitees after the closing date. Other schools may take several days or even a week or more to make their selection. I have heard even of a month, in circumstances where the financial situation of the school meant that they were unsure at first whether they could afford to fill the post.

If you have the interview date, or at least the interview week, it gives you an overview of their timescale. Generally, schools try to give candidates 3 or 4 days to request permission to attend the interview and prepare their observed lesson, although I know of one teacher who read at breakfast an e-mail sent at 4 in the morning inviting her to an interview that same day. Clearly a last-minute substitution for a candidate who had withdrawn. You might think that in those circumstances, she had little chance of being appointed, but in fact she was.

Normally you should not give up hope until 2 or 3 days before the interview date. And normally you should begin your interview preparation as soon as you have sent off your application, so that you are ready to go when the invitation comes. Please do this.

NEW SEPTEMBER 2022: SELF-DECLARATION

From 1st September 2022, the statutory guidance document ***Keeping children safe in education 2022 Statutory guidance for schools and colleges*** states the following:

Shortlisting

Shortlisted candidates should be asked to complete a self-declaration of their criminal record or information that would make them unsuitable to work with children. Self-declaration is subject to Ministry of Justice guidance on the disclosure of criminal records, further information can be found on GOV.UK

For example:

• if they have a criminal history

• if they are included on the children's barred list

• if they are prohibited from teaching

• if they are prohibited from taking part in the management of an independent school

• information about any criminal offences committed in any country in line with the law as applicable in England and

Wales, not the law in their country of origin or where they were convicted

· if they are known to the police and children's local authority social care

· if they have been disqualified from providing childcare (see paras 263-267), and,

· any relevant overseas information.

This information should only be requested from applicants who have been shortlisted. The information should not be requested in the application form to decide who should be shortlisted.

Applicants should be asked to sign a declaration confirming the information they have provided is true. Where there is an electronic signature, the shortlisted candidate should physically sign a hard copy of the application at point of interview.

The purpose of a self-declaration is so that candidates will have the opportunity to share relevant information and allow this to be discussed and considered at interview before the DBS certificate is received.

You should therefore be prepared to answer these questions once you are invited to interview.

HOW DO YOU REPLY
TO THE INVITATION?

It's very important that you reply to the invitation to interview; you might be so excited that you forget this. You should not reply, however, until you have received permission to attend – see the next chapters.

Send your reply by e-mail, having read carefully all the details. Thank them, and confirm that you will be attending. Tell them if you need any special consideration; for example, if you have a mobility problem that makes it difficult to climb stairs, you could ask for rooms to be on the ground floor or on a floor serviced by a lift. If you have a query about the observed lesson, ask this, but do not overload them with a long list of questions. Nor even a short list; just one or two if absolutely essential. Do not believe those who tell you that at every stage (from pre-application visit to the last minute of the interview) it is essential to ask questions in order to prove your commitment. Asking questions for the sake of it? Please don't do this.

WHAT IF YOU HAVE A CLASH OF INTERVIEWS?

L ike buses, interviews sometimes come along in twos – or threes. And sometimes you receive two invitations for an interview on the same day. What do you do then? It is tricky, very tricky.

First, you consider the logistics. Might it be possible to attend both, one in the morning and one in the afternoon, if timings were amended? If they are both in the same town, this might be feasible. If so, then speak to both the schools, explain the dilemma, and see if they would be amenable to changing their timings to accommodate you. You might be lucky, and there is always the fact that knowing that something is in demand by someone else works on the human psyche to make it more attractive to others.

If this is clearly impractical, or they decline, then you have to decide which one you would be willing to give up if you needed to. You then contact this school and ask if it would be possible to hold your interview on another day. Again, knowing that another school is interested in you and might steal you from under their nose will often encourage a school to be flexible here for you.

From their point of view, it would be better to see you the

day before the other candidates; seeing you the day after would mean making the other candidates wait a day longer to hear the result, which would be unfair on them (all that extra nail biting). It could also mean that they lose out on their favoured candidate if in the meantime s/he gets offered another job during that waiting period while they are interviewing you.

If they are unwilling or unable to accommodate this request for a change of day (and there are indeed often good logistical reasons for a school not to agree), then you will just have to withdraw from the interview. Make sure that you show that it is regretfully, writing a nice letter or e-mail thanking them for inviting you. You want to be in their good books in case you ever wish to apply there again; you would not want their reaction to the next application to be: *That's that awful chap who was so rude when we couldn't change his interview date when the Head had a hospital appointment the day before!*

WHAT IF YOU HAVE TWO INTERVIEWS, YOUR F AVOURITE LATER THAN A LESS ATTRACTIVE ONE?

This can crop up fairly often, especially in May when there are a number of interviews being held in the same weeks as schools rush to appoint before the resignation deadline of May 31. You have an interview for Tuesday for a fixed-term post, then you get another interview for later in the week for a permanent post, and at a school where the commute is much better too.

Your first innocent (but incorrect) reaction might be that you can go to the first interview, and if you are offered it, accept the post. Then you go to the second interview and if you are offered that one too, accept it and quickly withdraw your acceptance from the first one. After all, you haven't signed a contract, have you?

This innocent reaction (and an understandable reaction

– after all, you are not a Human Resources expert) is incorrect for a number of reasons. I am not a HR expert either, let alone an employment lawyer, but here is my (amateur) take on the situation. In my view, you have in fact entered into a contract with the first school – let us call it school A. You see, a verbal contract is binding (although it may be conditional on, for example, a DBS check or health declaration) on both parties; they made an offer and you accepted it. If you then pull out, you may be in breach of contract.

A further complication is that once you are contractually bound to school A, you are theoretically not free to make another contract with school B, so should not even go to their interview. This means that if you are offered a job with school A, and then decide to accept it, you must withdraw your application to school B. You cannot do what you would most wish to do: accept the job at school A, as an insurance offer rather like UCAS offers for university places, then go to school B, get that job, only to turn round and reject the job at school A after all.

When we consider it from the point of view of the school, it all makes sense. They have gone to the expense and effort of advertising and interviewing. They offer a job to candidate X. If X decides after a few days to turn it down, then they offer to Y. But unfortunately for them, candidate Y in the meantime has accepted another job offer, and they are left teacherless. This is what schools fear.

Because of this, most schools will offer the job by phone that evening or the next day, and expect an immediate answer to allow them to rush an offer to Y if X turns it down. Some schools offer on interview day there and then, and expect an immediate answer. I know of several schools who put a written offer letter in front of the candidate and get them to sign an acceptance on the spot; I have on just one occasion done it myself with an outstanding candidate that I did not want to lose.

So, would they be willing to wait for your answer to their offer until you have gone to the other interview in two or three days' time? Not very likely, as the very most that you could hope for would be 24 hours to think it over, I'm afraid. You should also be aware that some schools actually ask you at interview if you would accept the job if it were offered you.

Bear in mind too that if it is near a resignation deadline (31 October, 28/9 February, 31 May), schools will be very nervous about letting you have any thinking time at all, not even 24 hours, for fear of losing their second-choice candidate if they delay. This means that you need to have thought through all the pros and cons before accepting the interview – or indeed, before even applying. To turn round at this late stage and say that you need time to discuss the practicalities with your partner is really not on. You risk the school immediately withdrawing their offer in order to give it to their second choice.

So, what could happen to you if you did break a verbal contract by turning down the job with school A after accepting it? Several things could result. You would certainly get a poor reputation locally (by which I mean that school A's headteacher is likely to complain to your current headteacher, and probably mention it at the local meeting of headteachers). Also, school B would be justified in withdrawing their offer when they heard about it, not only because they feel that you have acted unprofessionally in accepting then declining the first offer, but also because you fraudulently led them to believe that you were able to enter into a contract with them (i.e. accept their offer) when in fact you were already contracted to school A. If school A are left really in the lurch, have to re-advertise etc., there is a possibility that they could try to sue you to re-coup their additional expenses.

You could be left with no job and a court case hanging over you. It is not very likely that all of that would happen, but even if only some of it did, it would not be a good situation for you. So, you have to decide how desperate you are to get another job; can you risk not getting one at all by declining the interview at school A and putting all your eggs into the basket of school B? If so, decline School A politely before interview. You should also try to consider how likely you are to get the job at school B.

You are probably thinking that this is all just theory, highly unlikely to happen, they would just accept your withdrawal with a cross word. No big deal, really. Just think about it again from a different perspective.

Let us suppose that you got an offer and accepted it from school B; the permanent post that you had been hoping for, you are very happy. Then a week later, you got a letter from school B saying that they had since interviewed someone else who suited them better, so were withdrawing the offer to you. How would you feel? So I think that you can understand what I mean when I say that that verbal contract in the phone call is binding on them, and binding on you.

My advice would be to go to the first interview; you can then decide whether or not you think that this is a school where you could happily work. If you decide that it is, then sit tight and hope for the good phone call, after which you withdraw from the interview at school B. If later that day, before the phone call, you decide, on reflection, that you would not wish to work in school A, then ring the school and tell them straight away that you are withdrawing, so that they do not waste time offering it to you (if that had been their intention, which it might not have been of course) but can go straight to making an offer to another candidate.

I will add that if at any time during the day at school A you feel that this is not the school for you, then you should withdraw immediately, and not go through with the interview. *You should do this with any interview that you attend.* This saves your time and above all it saves theirs too.

It means of course that you do not get the interview experience that you hoped for. I have heard of candidates withdrawing after a negative experience in the observed lesson, and then being indignant that they weren't given an interview despite having withdrawn, believing that they somehow had a right to professional development at the expense of a school that they had rejected.

Withdraw politely, saying that you realise that you are not the right teacher for this school (N.B. do not say that this is not the right school for you); you never know when you may meet that same headteacher again in a new professional context. ***Never burn your professional boats***.

The next step after having been shortlisted is asking permission to attend the interview.

3. ASKING FOR TIME OFF TO GO TO AN INTERVIEW

You may not realise that you cannot go to an interview without the headteacher's permission. If you are the headteacher, then it should be the chair of governors that you approach over this. The norm is that you are allowed to go to an interview for another job, and without losing any pay, but do take care how you word the request so that it does not sound like a demand.

Because it is a request, as a headteacher usually does not have to give you paid leave – or any leave – to go to an interview. I know that some of you believe that you have an unalienable right to three days off a year for going to interviews, but that is, in general, just a union recommendation (if you are under redundancy notice, the case is different). Some local authorities and governing bodies may indeed have an agreement specifically allowing teachers up to three days per year as paid leave for interviews in reasonable circumstances. But most do not have any such agreement, so you do need permission from the headteacher to attend an interview. This means going and asking politely, rather than merely sending an e-mail saying: *Just to let you know that my classes will need cover on Wednesday as I have an interview for a new job at Eton College.*

Normally your request will be granted, and even in those

schools where you do not have an entitlement to any paid days for interviews, most headteachers will allow you to go to more than three interviews, with one proviso: that the timing is not bad for pupils or for the school.

That is a very important point. Although usually you get the day off, and paid not unpaid, a headteacher may decide that it is not reasonable for you to be absent that particular day, because of the specific need of the school to have you there teaching. Perhaps several other staff are absent, perhaps it is an important time of the year for pupils, perhaps Ofsted is in.

A few teachers might consider taking the time off by pretending to be ill. Please do not do that. For a teaching job, where the reference will be requested before the interview, you couldn't deceive your school anyway, as they would suspect that your illness was just too conveniently timed. There could be a temptation to try this for a post outside teaching, where they are often happy to call for references after the interview. A teacher could ring in sick to go to the interview in secret in those circumstances.

However, this could be considered gross misconduct, so do not do it. Are you perhaps unsure what this means? Gross misconduct is a single act of misconduct that is serious enough on its own to justify an employee's immediate dismissal, with no pay in lieu of notice. So that is why you would be extremely unwise to do this.

If a teacher were to defraud the school by taking the day off without permission, the possible consequences could be that s/he would lose a day's pay, would be subject to disciplinary procedures, probably for gross misconduct, and the current employer would write to the other school to inform them, so that the teacher could end up with no job at all.

So what should you do? Once you have received the invitation to go to the interview, tell your KS co-ordinator or head of department about the invitation, and see what possible suggestions there are for covering your classes. It is not your responsibility, but it is always courteous and helpful to colleagues to have prepared the lesson plans (simple ones!) for the missing classes, together with the resources needed. Then go to see the headteacher's secretary, say that you have come to ask permission to go to an interview, so could you have an appointment. The response may be *Oh that's OK – you don't need to tell him/her in person, I'll let him/her know.* In case this is so, do have ready a brief polite note that you can hand over, requesting permission and saying that lesson plans and materials will be left for the day.

In every stage of the application – interview – resignation process, courtesy to both schools is the over-riding rule.

4. THE AIMS OF THE INTERVIEW FOR A CANDIDATE

The aims of the interview for the panel I deal with further on. For you as candidate you may think that there is only one aim and it is quite clear: it is to get the job offer. But in fact there are two aims for you. Firstly, it must be to get the offer of a job that is appropriate for you in a context in which you can work effectively and happily. And secondly, it is not to get sacked once appointed. Not to get sacked for dishonesty or because you just aren't up to the job, because you cannot walk the talk.

Both these aims involve honesty. If you present yourself in the interview as someone that you are not (often because you have learnt someone else's answers and responses), then the person that they are appointing is not the real you, but someone that you were pretending to be. And the real you may turn out to be a square peg in a round hole, and not at all happy in the job. A horrible situation. So do not pretend, just present yourself honestly as you truly are.

The second point is not just about presenting yourself as one thing when in fact your true character is different, it is about actually lying and deliberately deceiving the appointment panel. It is, for example, claiming qualifications or experience that you do not possess. If you do this and are subsequently found out, then you could not only be summarily dismissed for dishonesty or be subject to capability proceedings for inability to carry out the job, but also in some cases become liable to criminal proceedings.

Honesty in all things. This should be the over-arching personal theme of the whole interview experience

5. OTHER ACTIVITIES AS PART OF THE SELECTION PROCESS

The interview is not the only activity that is set up as part of the selection process. The other common ones include an observed lesson, a visit round the school, a student panel, and meeting the rest of the department or key stage team for coffee or even for lunch, and perhaps a short presentation to the interview panel. There is occasionally also a written task to carry out, one that is directly related to the post for which you are applying, so a classroom teacher would have something very different from a candidate for head of department.

Depending on the timing of these different activities for the different candidates, it is usually possible for all of you to arrive together and meet as a group to be welcomed by the headteacher and given a cup of school coffee. At this stage (or indeed at any other stage), do not try to stand out from the crowd. A colleague tells the story of the candidate who asked the head over the welcoming cup of coffee: *Could you tell us what brought you into teaching, and what is your personal philosophy of education?* Totally inappropriate to ask a question like that. Very unwise to try and impress. That was one candidate immediately out of the competition, was the immediate reaction of the more astute interviewees.

A special note to prospective senior leaders here: do not see the initial group meeting over coffee with the head/chair of governors, or indeed the tour of the school, as a talking contest. Headteachers in particular are not seeking, when appointing an assistant or deputy head, someone who can dominate conversations or push themselves forward. Often, listening interestedly is the best policy.

After the coffee, you are now about to begin the serious activities of the day; you may have been given your personal schedule for the day beforehand, or it may be handed out now, listing the different activities that you will complete.

THE OBSERVED LESSON

T eaching a lesson at interview should be the easier part of the selection experience, as it is something that you do day in, day out, and feel confident about. In addition, candidates who are students still working towards gaining their qualification are accustomed to regular observations, so should not feel too uncomfortable about this.

Use your normal planning document, and come with several copies of your plan that you can thrust into the hand of the observer – or observers if there is more than one, as there sometimes are two people looking at different aspects. If it has been a while since you've been observed or inspected formally, you may care to remind yourself of the planning basics. Or indeed of some of the bells and whistles. These two books will be of general use to you as a teacher, and are worth buying now. N.B., I get nothing for recommending them. The first is by Isabella Wallace and Leah Kirkman, and is called *Pimp your Lesson*. The second, by Jackie Beere, is called *The Perfect (Ofsted) Lesson*. There are also specific Perfect Lesson books for Maths and English. These are all available from Amazon, as are many other similar books. Browse and look at several before you make up your mind which seems to suit you best.

I cannot compete with those experts in lesson planning, but I can give you a few general tips for the observed lesson as part of the interview process.

If you feel that you do not have enough information about the class, do contact the school by e-mail to enquire more.

But do not send an enormous list of questions.

Ensure that your lesson is focused on objectives, not activities. Even if you think that you have a great activity, don't do it; choose the objectives first and then the activities. Avoid at all costs trying to find objectives that fit the activity that you have already chosen.

Do not have a lesson that relies entirely on technology. Yours may not be compatible with theirs, or theirs may fail.

Have a Plan B if there is any technology at all planned in your lesson.

Do not assume that they will have materials available. Bring your own.

Do not be extravagant with materials or resources; you may not be able to have that level of spending if appointed.

The TA is a valuable resource in primary schools. Ask if one will be there, and have a clear role for him/her.

Remember to have differentiation clearly marked in your lesson plan, in case you don't get a chance to implement it.

Have an extra section at the end of your plan, where you suggest what the follow-up should be.

Try to gauge the probable level of the class by looking at the published examination results of the school. If they are substantially higher or lower than your current experience, adjust your lesson accordingly.

Do not stick to your plan like grim death. If it is clear that you have got the level wrong, adapt it immediately to suit the needs of the pupils.

Therefore, come with a Plan B and a Plan C at different levels, just in case.

But your Plan B or Plan C should not be playing Hangman, as advocated by the book that I quoted at the beginning.

Be prepared, in the interview, to say what went well, how you know it went well, and what you might change another time.

There is another, very important, piece of advice about the observed lesson. It is this: plan, devise and prepare the lesson yourself. Specifically, do not go on to popular online education forums and ask for help, suggestions or ideas, and do not use the lesson plans or ideas that are available for teachers on the internet.

Not even the TES Resources; great as they are for everyday use, they are not suitable for interview lessons. Not the paid resources, not the free ones, not any of them.

This is because the school to which you are applying does not just want to see you teach. If they did, they would issue you with a lesson plan and materials to use. They also wish to see if you can plan a lesson appropriately and then deliver it effectively. Deliver your lesson, yours, the one that you thought up and planned yourself.

And here are two cautionary tales in case you are thinking of ignoring this advice and going ahead with this great lesson that you have already downloaded from the TES Resources, or anywhere else.

In the days when the TES forums existed, one headteacher read the forum replies giving ideas and a lesson plan in answer to a plea for help with preparing an observed lesson for a primary interview. She then recognised the lesson a few days later when it was given at her school. It wouldn't have mattered much, actually, if she hadn't happened to read the forum replies and recognised it, because no fewer than four, four of the six candidates, used the very same lesson. This reminds us that anything on the internet may have been read by other candidates or by the interview panel themselves. Do not go there. Plan your own.

The other cautionary tale involves actual deception. For a secondary English/drama post, there was one lesson which was extremely well planned, and used excellent resources. When questioned about the planning process, and where the idea came from for the materials, the candidate blustered her way through, although not very convincingly. What she did not know was that the lesson, and the materials, had been devised and posted in the TES Resources by the Deputy Head who was part of the appointment panel and was questioning her about them.

The TES forums no longer exist, but the TES Resources still do, as do other online resources. You never know when another candidate has chosen the same online lesson plan as you. You never know when you might meet the author of work that you claim as your own. Do not go there. Plan your own.

Some schools filter out candidates after the lesson observation; this can be very disappointing, even upsetting, but there is no point in staying on if your teaching style does not match theirs. Sometimes you, too, may decide to withdraw after this lesson, if your experience has been such that it is clear that this is not the environment for you to work in. Be polite, say nothing negative about the school or its pupils, and do not expect to be given interview practice for your personal professional development.

VISIT ROUND THE SCHOOL

Y ou may have had a formal or informal visit to the school before applying; this is discussed in my book *Applying for a Teaching Job 2022-3*. Many schools also have a timetable for candidates on interview that includes a walk around the school, accompanied by either a member of staff or pupils.

There is a dual aim here. Firstly, this is your chance to use your eyes and ears and decide if this is the context in which you could work effectively and happily. Eyes and ears more than mouth – do not overload your guide with questions, and ask nothing negative. You can ask pupils what it is that they like best about the school, but it is best not to ask them what they like least, or what is the worst thing about the school.

Secondly, you are on interview during this visit, but on interview as a person, not as a teacher. Smile, be pleasant and polite, comment favourably without being over-effusive, and do not try to impress. Note one or two positives so that if, in the interview, you are asked about the visit, you are ready to respond. You may sometimes be asked what you would like to change; try to think of something relatively minor, and for which the school, especially the SLT, bears no blame.

STUDENT PANEL

From 1st September 2022, the statutory guidance document ***Keeping children safe in education 2022 Statutory guidance for schools and colleges*** states the following:

> *Pupils/students should be involved in the recruitment process in a meaningful way. Observing short listed candidates and appropriately supervised interaction with pupils/students is common and recognised as good practice.*

The student panel – it may be the school's Student Council – will have been well prepared by staff beforehand. Disruptive elements will have been excluded (they want you to be impressed by their students) and the questions to ask you will have been vetted carefully to avoid surprises of the *Sir! Sir! Have you got a girlfriend!* type from primary, or a query about your politics from secondary.

You may nonetheless get some of the daft questions which come into and out of fashion. Things like: *If you were a biscuit/car/animal, which would you be?* If you get one of these weird questions, think of your best quality, and then decide which biscuit/car/animal best illustrates this. This is hard to do on the spot, so decide now what your quality is (dependable, supportive, caring, sporty, creative, etc) and then try and think of biscuit/car/animal to match. Good luck with that!

Remember that this panel, like the formal interview panel, will have its BBs, its buying buttons. These were discussed in *Applying for a Teaching Job 2022-3*, and we'll look at them again later on in the context of the preparation for the interview. Try and decide what these BBs will be, what is important for pupils of this age (bullying including cyberbullying may well be one of them), so that you can do a mind map of them as preparation if you are told that there will be a student panel. The mind map done of the BBs for the first interview will serve for subsequent schools, as these are unlikely to change much, so it's a one-off task. More about this later in the section on the right preparation

Finally, ensure that you remain friendly but professional; do not try to be over-familiar nor matey. You are not their mate nor even their friend or older sibling; you are a teacher who sets standards and is a role model. Keep your language entirely appropriate and professional. Similarly, if any child says anything inappropriate, do what any teacher should do and softly challenge it, or dismiss with "That's not really a suitable topic for discussion here, is it?"

MEETING
COLLEAGUES

In a maintained school, you are unlikely to be subjected to *Trial by Sherry Party* and its older brother *Trial for self and partner by Dinner Party*. These are reserved for candidates – generally for SLT posts - at independent schools. Meeting your prospective colleagues for coffee or for lunch – with the other candidates also present – is fairly common, however. Eating under these circumstances can be challenging, especially as nerves tend to dull the appetite; if this is the case for you, a headteacher friend of mine recommends the 'put a few things on your plate and push them around in the manner of actors on TV' method.

Another headteacher says: "When I was called for interview for my present headship in a Catholic school, I was subjected to their younger sister, *Trial by Tea Party*. It was quite an experience! They wanted to see how I interacted with colleagues, and how I would fit into the team that I would lead."

Here the aim is to be seen as a pleasant and supportive colleague who would fit well into the team. Smile, be friendly, do not interrogate colleagues about the school and its drawbacks. Ask curriculum questions if appropriate, but do not labour this. Especially do not try to outshine or outshout the other candidates, and above all, do not try to impress. You may think that I labour this non-impression; let me tell you that candidates can talk themselves out of a job before reaching the interview room by trying ostentatiously to impress.

For a MFL position, you may find that the native speaker(s) in the department waylay you to give you what amounts to a brief oral examination to check your fluency and accent.

WRITTEN TASK

This is not seen in every interview. Any written task will be specifically targeted at what would be the sort of task carried out in the normal duties of the post. It is not to be feared, as it is always eminently do-able; there would be no point whatsoever in setting a task so complex or difficult that candidates could not carry it out. My main advice would be to keep calm about it, read the instructions carefully, and use your time wisely. Just what we say to the students!

So, normal tasks for that post; this could include:

Writing a letter to parents to introduce yourself as the new class teacher (primary)

Doing a grammar test (KS2)

Planning a lesson

Drafting in outline a unit of work for part of the curriculum

Marking a piece of work and setting targets for improvement

Interpreting class data

Interpreting whole-school data with feedback on three priorities identified (SLT)

Writing a letter refusing a request for pupil holiday in term time (headteacher)

Answering an A-level question (I have known this in maths and sciences)

In-tray with a series of tasks to prioritise and write notes on (middle and senior leaders rather than classroom posts)

Short presentation to the interview panel

I'll comment at this point only on the last one. If you are asked to do a presentation, it may seem nerve-racking (or even nerve-wrecking), but it is not much different from teaching. Normally you do it right at the start of the interview, and then there are a few questions about it before they swing into the interview proper.

My advice is that you are very careful about the timing; normally you are asked only for 5 minutes for classroom teachers, perhaps 10 minutes for leaders. Do not try to pack too much in, as you should be speaking fairly slowly and deliberately rather than gabbling. Practice it at home and time it – often they will stop you mid-sentence when your time is up, so try for 15 or 30 seconds less.

Keep it clear and simple; the advice for a short talk is: *Tell'em what you are going to tell'em; tell'em it; tell'em what you told'em.* In other words, three clear sections: an introduction, main section and a summary/conclusion.

Do not bother with a PowerPoint if it's only 5 minutes, have at the very most a small card with a few main points on it, and speak from your heart. Remember to smile and make eye contact with the panel as you speak.

And please do not ask for ideas on an online forum – get your own ideas so that they reflect you, your values, who and what you are.

WITHDRAWING BEFORE THE INTERVIEW

I f after, or even during, any of these activities, you decide that this is not the school for you, then the courteous thing to do is to withdraw and not go forward to the interview. I must warn you that some misguided schools impose punitive damages on you, and refuse to pay your travel expenses if you withdraw. This should have been set out in the documents that you received about the interview and expenses. Very many schools pay little in the way of travel expenses nowadays, so it may be no great loss.

6. THE INTERVIEW PANEL

I nterviews for teaching posts in schools, academies and colleges normally involve a panel of people. This may not always be the case in an interview for a post at an independent school – more about that later on. A panel is considered best practice in the maintained sector, with three or more people involved, although for leadership posts it can be many more, perhaps even the whole of the governing body for a headship.

The members of the panel will usually include the person who will be the direct line manager for the post; this may be a head of department, a pastoral leader or a key stage co-ordinator. There will be at least one member of the senior leadership team, normally the headteacher. It is not necessary to have a governor on a panel for a classroom teacher post, which is lucky really, as their diaries are often so full that scheduling the interviews can be tricky. However, for headteacher and other senior leadership posts there will always be governors, possibly someone from the local authority or academy trust, and also perhaps a consultant – someone like me.

Having said that, as governors are the employers in most Catholic schools, it is prudent to expect that there will be one or more governors present on the interview panel for any post in a Catholic school. Governors are often not as au fait with the education jargon and acronyms as other panel members; it is important to bear this in mind in your answers.

Before the interview the panel will meet to discuss the format of the interview (who asks questions when) and its content (which questions to ask). The panel will look at the job description and person specification and then devise questions which enable them to test whether a candidate fits their requirements. A decision will be made on who asks which question in which order.

In order to ensure fair appointment procedures, these standard questions will normally be asked of each candidate; however as noted earlier, the newer types of schools sometimes drive a coach and horses through notions of 'fair recruitment', so don't be surprised to find, on swapping experiences, that you are asked different questions from other candidates. If all candidates are asked the same questions, you may think that in that case there is no point in having a panel interview – all the candidates could just as well sit down in the language laboratory and record their answers digitally. However, although the primary questions will normally be the same, any secondary and follow-up questions will be different for each candidate.

And, of course, the way that you answer, the way that you relate to the panel, will be judged too.

THE AIMS OF THE INTERVIEW FOR THE PANEL

The over-arching guidelines for interview panels are set out in: ***Keeping children safe in education 2022 Statutory guidance for schools and colleges, 1 September 2022.***

Selection

Schools and colleges should use a range of selection techniques to identify the most suitable person for the post. Those interviewing should agree structured questions. These should include:

• finding out what attracted the candidate to the post being applied for and their motivation for working with children

• exploring their skills and asking for examples of experience of working with children which are relevant to the role, and,

• probing any gaps in employment or where the candidate has changed employment or location frequently, asking about the reasons for this.

These are clearly important parts of the interview process that the panel must bear in mind. If you are reading this book because you are on an interview panel, think carefully with your colleagues how to achieve these. If you are a candidate, think how to show the panel that you can help them achieve their aims. There are above already at least four areas for you to prepare.

I begin any meeting of an appointment panel that I chair by reminding my colleagues of our three overriding aims of the day. The first aim is not to get sued for discriminatory or unfair practice, the second aim is to appoint the best possible candidate, one that meets the needs of the school. If that candidate is not here today, I add, then we do not appoint. And finally, our aim is to give each candidate such a pleasant experience and such a favourable impression of the school that they go home and tell everyone: *I am very sorry that I didn't get appointed – it seems an excellent place to work.* It is our opportunity to do an effective PR job on a group of five or six people, and spread our good reputation by word of mouth.

SOME THINGS THAT YOU PROBABLY DO NOT KNOW ABOUT THE INTERVIEW PANEL

The interview panel is often made up of people who, with the exception of the chair, are not very experienced in interviewing. How often does a head of history in your school appoint a new colleague? And they are certainly not professionals at this game. So unless they are tightly controlled by having the standard questions clearly worded, they may ask poor questions, such as a hypothetical question that could allow an invented answer, or anything beginning: *Have you ever . . .* This latter type of question is poor, of course, because it can elicit a one-word response: yes or no.

HOW TO COPE WITH INAPPROPRIATE QUESTIONS

Apart from some possible training in safeguarding and child protection, obligatory for only one person (the 2009 staffing regulations require one member of every selection panel to have received training on safer recruitment to help them identify and reject unsuitable candidates), most of the panel will have received no training for this role in interviewing prospective teachers. It is up to the headteacher or whoever else is chairing the panel to ensure that they know what the legal parameters are, especially regarding the protected characteristics under the Equality Act, to avoid the embarrassing situation when a panel member asks a question that should never be asked, usually regarding age, or family commitments. Not long ago in a large and prestigious independent school in London, a candidate was asked about her family, and then: *As a single mother of two, how will you juggle the demands of this job and looking after your family?*

The blame for that lies squarely on the chair of the panel, who should have stepped in immediately the first question was asked about the family, preventing the candidate from answering and thus preventing the follow-up question.

I have had personal experience of an inappropriate

question. In an interview for a headship where the institution had just gone co-educational, the girls still working their way through the year groups, I was asked: *If you are appointed, and as head you come to the annual Old Boys' Dinner, how will you feel about being the only woman in the room?* Slight pause, before he continued: *Apart from the waitresses, of course.* This question was asked by the chair of governors, who had earlier started off the proceedings by coming into the room where all the candidates were waiting and saying, looking at me: *Right, I think we'll kick off with Blondie. What's your name, my dear?*

This was over twenty years ago; I'd like to think that this wouldn't happen nowadays, but the example quoted earlier shows that it might. So what should you do if you are asked an inappropriate question in the interview?

Your first port of call must be the chair, who should know that this is inappropriate, so turn ostentatiously and look at him or her with a blank face, showing no emotion at all. This should not even be necessary, as s/he should have stepped in immediately and said: *I think that we'll move on from that question, Peter; I believe it is now Jane's turn to ask something of our candidate?* But if this does not happen, and s/he does not take the hint from your blank stare, you have a choice between answering the question very briefly: *I'm 26*, or answering with an addition: *I'm 26, although I am sure that age is not a criterion for this post*, or not answering the question, merely saying: *I'm not sure that this is a criterion for this post.*

Whichever you do, it will be upsetting for you as a candidate, and potentially off-putting during an already stressful interview experience. It could also be the subject of an official complaint to the school. If you do consider going down this route, consult your union.

If you are reading this as a member of an interview panel, please be aware of your responsibilities here.

THE PANEL IS PROBABLY INEXPERIENCED, UNTRAINED AND NERVOUS

So, the panel will mainly be inexperienced, mainly be untrained, and also mainly be very nervous. They will be more nervous than you in many cases. Why are they so nervous? They are nervous because they are inexperienced; they are nervous because they are worried about what impression they are making on the other people on the panel; they are nervous or even frightened of making a fool of themselves, frightened of picking the wrong person, frightened they won't be able to appoint anyone at all.

As a result of their nerves and fears, the panel are on your side. They want you to be good, to prove that they were right in shortlisting you, and above all, they want you to be good so they can appoint you; their worst nightmare is not appointing, and having to do it all again. You are the one in a strong position here.

So the first Do's and Don'ts are:

Do be positive in your thinking and in your responses.

Don't get nervous of the panel - remember – they want to find a reason to appoint you.

I am going to talk to you about Do's and Don'ts in general, give you some techniques for answering questions, my advice for preparation and talk about other aspects of the process so that you can feel confident and give the very best of yourself in the interview for that all-important job.

7. THE INTERVIEW – GENERAL OVERVIEW

This and the following sections will deal with various aspects of school and college interviews in general. There is an additional full section on senior leadership interviews later on; however, *SLT candidates should also read this section, as they need the information and advice in here.*

The school will have arranged a schedule for the interviews to ensure that every candidate gets to teach, to visit the school, to carry out any other activity before the formal interview. This is to allow some discussion of this to take place in the interview. It is helpful if they also take into consideration travelling times for the different candidates, so that those who have furthest to travel are not the last to leave.

Candidates normally have a room, supplied with water and biscuits permanently, with coffee and tea being offered at intervals, where they can sit when not otherwise engaged, and while waiting for their interview. Someone will come to collect each candidate when the panel is ready for them.

It is important that this room is both comfortable and private; the candidates may spend quite some time here between the various activities on their schedule. I was once interviewed for a headship along with three other candidates, one of whom was the acting headteacher. He sat in solitary comfort in his generously-sized head's office. The two other candidates and I sat on hard classroom chairs lined up against the back wall of the cramped office of the head of year 9, who was using her office to interview students about their GCSE options or personal problems all the time that we were there. Yes, the acting headteacher was appointed, but then left by mutual agreement after one year. No, I did not apply the next time that the vacancy arose.

When you go into the interview room, smile. Then shake hands if this is offered; try wiping your right hand discreetly on your clothes in the corridor as you walk to the room, to dry it if you are nervous. The chair of the panel, who will normally be the headteacher that you met first thing, will ask generally you what name you prefer to use; it may be an abbreviation of your first name or a second name; do not give a nickname nor an abbreviation harking back to childhood, keep everything professional.

The chair will then introduce the other members of the panel, saying briefly what their role is. You then sit down and it begins.

When I am chairing an interview, I start by explaining to the candidate that I am going to talk for a few minutes to explain the selection process and the format of the interview. The difficulties of doing this in reported speech are such that I shall just write out roughly what I say, in note form. I imagine that many other interviews begin in a similar way.

Welcome – we hope you enjoyed the visit round the school. Thank you for time spent on application, which impressed us, and for coming today.

Aim of the interview is twofold: us getting the right person for school, and you getting the right school for you – dual selection. Important point: if you feel that it isn't right for you, you can withdraw now, or later, and we shall still pay your travel expenses. You are selecting us, too.

Selection procedures: we select based on Application + Task (presentation and observed lesson) + Examination Results for your groups over last 3 years + References + Interview. So interview important.

Format of interview: Qs from us all in this order (name panel). I begin and end the interview.

This interview is designed to give you your chance to show us you are best candidate.

We have devised questions, based on the job description and person specification, that give everyone an equal opportunity to show us that they are indeed the best candidate.

Therefore same lead Q's for all candidates (some supplementary Q's may be different, as based on your answers or your application).

3 Standard Qs at end (Anything else you'd like to say in support of your application; Any urgent questions for us; Are you still interested in post?). When you hear these, you'll know that you are on the home stretch! If you forget to say something at any one point, or we don't ask the question that would have given you chance to tell us something important, you'll have that chance at the end to add something else in your support.

We shall ring everyone this evening with the result. Any offer subject to statutory checks, checks of qualifications, satisfactory references, and proof of right to reside and work in UK according to the relevant Asylum & Immigration Act. That's the legal bit! Salary TBA   N.B. we shall take notes.

Have you any queries about the interview process? Is it all clear? Shall we start now?

In an attempt to put the candidates at their ease, I try to have open body language and speak warmly, not too formally. Nobody wants the candidates to be so stressed that they cannot do their best, and panels try to de-stress as much as possible. We have water on the table in front of the candidate, but not tea or coffee, as it is more distressing for a candidate if s/he spills that.

I once had a candidate who, at the end of my little speech, said: *Actually, I am an illegal immigrant, since I don't have the right to be here. Does this make a difference?* We halted the interview at that point, sent him to have a coffee and to talk to the Bursar to try to sort that out. Unfortunately for him, we couldn't.

The lead questions are very carefully thought out beforehand, so that we can explore to what extent the candidate meets our criteria and could carry out the job. By looking at the person specification and the job description for the post that you are applying for, you can make a good guess at the sort of things you will be asked about. More later on about deciding which will be the topics for the interview.

As chair, I begin and end the interview. My introductory question is designed to make the candidate feel more comfortable by telling me something positive. Most interviews start with a similar attempt to relieve the stress.

Introductory Questions: Tell us about a success. (Follow-up) What does this answer tell me about you?

Can you briefly describe the scope of your current job, and what motivated you to apply for this job?

At the end, just before the three standard questions that I told the candidate about, I ask a couple more questions. I ask: *How would your best friend describe you?* Sometimes I vary it by asking how colleagues would describe you. After you have answered, usually with some pretty positive remarks if you have any sense, I then repeat what you said and add: *But . . . ?*

This would come out something like this: *So you are hard-working, creative, supportive of colleagues and very committed to your job. But...?* Do not fall into this hole that I am laying out invitingly in front of you.

I have one final thing to say to the candidate in the interview, which is: *You told us at the beginning about your success in XXX, now tell us about a disaster.* Another hole dug deep right in front of you. Think of something that was not that bad, was some time ago in the past, tell us how you put it right, tell us what you learned from it, and it will all be to your credit as a reflective, developing practitioner of the art of teaching.

The worst – or best, depending on your point of view – response that I ever got at that point was from an IT teacher who described how, in a year 9 class, when he goes (note that – goes, goes regularly, not went on one occasion) out to fetch some worksheets he's left in the department office, or to make more photocopies, or to get the class notes that he forgot, the students always pull out screwdrivers and start taking the computers to pieces. He ended up by saying: *And they do it every single time!*

No, he wasn't offered a job.

We round up the interview with the three standard questions, then we thank the candidate and ask him/her to leave with the secretary a telephone number and a time when s/he would be available to be phoned with the result.

And we jolly well make sure that everyone is phoned when we said that we would.

8. THE 5 MISTAKES THAT TEACHERS MAKE IN AN INTERVIEW

By now you should have a good understanding of the process of selection. However, interviews are stressful, things can go wrong for you. But they can also go very right with the proper thought, attention and preparation, as you will learn in this book.

THE FIVE MISTAKES TO AVOID IN AN INTERVIEW

There are five general mistakes that candidates can make in an interview.

The wrong first impression

The wrong self-presentation

The wrong sort of talking

The wrong sort of preparation

The wrong questions at the end

9. THE WRONG FIRST IMPRESSION

You must give an impeccable impression of a professional right from the very first moment that you are on school premises. Start by reading very carefully all the information that you are sent about the interview, and ensure that you follow the instructions to the letter.

Arriving late and flustered from a difficult journey is not a good idea. If possible, that is if the school is fairly local, make the journey a day or two beforehand as a trial. This way you will know what to expect, where the bus stops are, how you get into the school car park, etc. You are unlikely to be able to do this in the same traffic conditions as on interview day, so make allowances for this. If a trial journey is not possible, at the very least you should travel there digitally with Google Street View.

Ensure that you have the school number correctly entered on your phone, that it is fully charged and with credit if PAYG, and enough cash to take an emergency taxi if necessary.

Check carefully the documents that you will need to bring, usually original copies of qualifications and some proof of identity. Ensure that you bring anything else that you may need: pens, pencils, paper handkerchiefs, spare tights, as well as everything that you need for your observed lesson. Bring a copy of your application with you, including your executive summary; also a small card with your USPs and their BBs for a quick reminder before you go in to the interview, not to actually take in and read from. If you are unsure about these last three, which are explained in full in my previous book ***Applying for a Teaching Job 2022-3***, I shall go over these briefly later on.

Be unfailingly courteous to everyone that you meet; this begins with reception staff. However awful your journey may have been, however nervous you may feel, the reception staff will be your first point of contact, and it is pretty common for them to be asked for their opinion of the way that the candidates introduced themselves and how they acted while waiting.

Turn off your phone just before you walk into the building. Not down to vibrate, not down to silent, but off. And then keep it off for all the time that you are on school premises. This will hopefully ensure that you don't automatically pull it out and look at the screen as you walk between activity sessions.

10. THE WRONG SELF-PRESENTATION

T his is where you must take especial care. You must present yourself as a professional teacher in every way.

How you dress for the interview is extremely important. You may well believe, and you may well be right, that how you dress has little impact on your effectiveness as a teacher. But it does have an impact on how you are perceived by the people who are appointing teachers. The overall impression that you make – and that means your personal presentation including how you are dressed – will always impact favourably or unfavourably on the appointment panel.

If you Google *First impressions interview*, you will come up with a myriad of websites telling you that people make up their mind about you in the first 30 seconds, 60 seconds or two minutes. Including making a decision about whether or not you are suitable for their post. So in fact, one of the most important parts of the interview is the first few minutes when you walk into the interview room.

Most interviewers know this and are alert to the fact that they mustn't be over-influenced by a candidate's appearance, but it is justifiable to consider that inappropriate personal presentation shows a lack of judgment that could rule you out as a suitable teacher in that school.

WHAT TO WEAR TO THE INTERVIEW

S o what is appropriate clothing for a teaching interview? In my view, the basic rule is this: *You are trying to be appointed, not invited out on a date.* By this I mean that you are trying to look professional, not attractive. For a job interview in any profession, an interview means going up a notch from what you would wear when actually in the job (so do not base your clothes on what you have observed the teachers wearing in that school), and certainly not wearing what you would on a date or an evening out with friends. Formal wear probably best describes it. I'm sorry if this makes you shudder.

For leadership posts, this means a suit, shirt and sober tie for men, and for women, skirt or dress/trousers and jacket. For teaching posts, men and women, a jacket is best for the interview, although you may wish to leave it off for the teaching. A shirt and tie – I insist not a novelty tie – for men, with a jacket. By this I mean a boring formal jacket, not a leather biker jacket nor a denim jacket. It does not have to be a suit, but a suit is good for both genders. For EYFS where you may sit on the floor and certainly lean over little tables, this probably means trousers for women.

If you teach P.E., you will need to bring a bag with a change of clothes, with the formal wear most of the time, gym wear for when you are teaching.

Some women, especially young women, may not feel comfortable in a jacket, as they are not used to them; there are, however, some soft knitted jackets that look smart and you can feel at ease in them. Women are advised to try out their whole outfit in front of a mirror, and try leaning forwards and seeing the image that this gives. Then imagine year 10 boys looking at this. Consider both the front (cleavage) and back (tightness of skirt or trousers) view that students would receive if you bent over a desk to look at a student's work.

Hair should be clean and tidy; long hair is best tied back – appointed, not dated, remember? Sitting casually throwing back your raven locks or golden curls from time to time is more suited to a bar than to an interview. Only light make-up should be worn, and discreet jewellery. Avoid anything flashy or dangly, and bracelets that could jangle or crash against a table edge. Hold back on the perfume and aftershave, and do not wear towering high heels or mules. I presume that I do not need to tell you not to wear trainers or Crocs, and that shoes should be clean and polished as appropriate.

If you have tattoos, it is best, if possible, to wear clothes that cover them, as these can be contrary to the dress code in some schools. The same applies to exotic piercings, by which I mean anything other than one earring in the lobe of each year.

I had a little chuckle when I read in another book on teaching interviews, aimed at the UK market this time, the following advice:

> What are their brand colours? You may wish to wear a tie or some other element of your clothing that symbolises the colour of the educational establishment. This is a subtle way of demonstrating your commitment to their brand and identity.

No, please do not. I would have more than a little chuckle if I went to join the candidates at the start of the day and saw many of them wearing the school uniform colours.

I know that this all sounds very boring, but this is the professional image that most interview panels are expecting. Imagine taking your Granny to lunch at a nice restaurant on her birthday, and wanting her to be really happy and pleased with you. That's the effect that you should be aiming for.

At this point you may be extremely unhappy with what I am saying. You may feel that it is your right to express your personality at all times, including in how you dress for an interview. Fair enough. But just remember that the interview panel also has the right not to choose you for their school.

I suggest that when you start job hunting, you identify what will be your interview outfit, including shoes and all underwear, and give it a thorough check. Are there any loose or any missing buttons, including on shirt cuffs? Any stains or unsewn seams? Is the hem undone, or the blouse too tight, and does your bra show through? Are the shoes scruffy, and will a good polish be enough to restore them? Do you need to buy a new tie, as the only ones you own are either greasy at the knot or stained, or not sober enough?

Talking of ties, nothing contentious is the rule. Sober, boring, not gaudy or novelty. And not like the tie that I once saw on a candidate. I had to make a real effort to listen to him and keep my eyes off the tie; it is always hard to concentrate on what a candidate is doing and saying when there is a visual distraction. It seemed to me to have a design of cannabis leaves, an impression that was subsequently confirmed by my colleagues after the interview. At the very end, as he was leaving, I commented: "*That's an interesting tie.*" "*Yes*", he replied proudly, "*I got it in Amsterdam.*" We gave him the benefit of the doubt here, and decided that he was wearing it in all innocence. Do not risk it, as you might not be so lucky.

Another point about the interview outfit, one that

concerns women. Some candidates, both male and female, when they are nervous come out almost instantly in a rash. This tends to start on your chest and move upwards. If you are wearing a low-necked top (I am not referring to anything very low cut, just a normal boat neckline, for example, or an open-necked shirt), then this bright red rash catches our eye and we watch, fascinated, as it moves up over your chest and up your neck to your face. This means that we are not paying attention to what you are saying.

If you know that you can suffer from this, it is best to have an attractive silky scarf round your neck, to hide the developing eye-riveting spectacle. Men's shirt collars done up with a tie do the job for them.

Once you have decided on the outfit, do try it on again. Including both the shoes. I say this because one candidate I know bought a new pair of shoes for an interview, went to put them on in the hotel, only to discover that one was a whole shoe size smaller than the other; he had clearly tried on only one shoe in the shop. The choice was scruffy trainers with the smart suit, or walking in agony all day long. He chose the latter, and still got the job. Wearing two shoes of the same size does not always guarantee this, of course.

If your outfit is formal, smart, clean and well-fitting, you will feel more confident. You will feel confident because you know that you look good, professional and in control.

DO THE SMELL TEST

F inally, test the outfit for smell. Better still, ask someone else to test it for you.

Smelling strongly of anything, even perfume, aftershave or cigarette smoke, is bad. Unwashed smell is even worse, and it may come from a candidate's clothes, not just from his or her unwashed body. I would say that in my experience, you get one case of BO in every three sets of interviews, say one out of 15-18 candidates interviewed. So it is not that unusual. When we have a candidate who smells, apart from not appointing that person, we have to have a pause in the interview procedure while the room is being aired before we can resume.

To be on the safe side, jackets, trousers and skirts should therefore be dry-cleaned if they are not new, and all other garments freshly washed. Once you have got the outfit ready, including getting it dry cleaned if necessary, put it away (with spare pair of tights to take with you for women) and keep it just for interviews. I shouldn't imagine that you'll want to wear it out clubbing anyway.

Identify too the bag to take with you. If you have a fashionably large handbag, you can get A4 folders in that, so do not need a briefcase. That means one less thing to struggle with and drop out of nerves. A headteacher friend has a very beautiful messenger bag which she uses for school visits and meetings, because it means that she doesn't need to carry both a handbag and a briefcase.

Remember: you are not trying to look attractive in an interview, you are trying to impress with your professionalism in all things. Beware of thinking *best clothes,* as for many young people in particular, best clothes are certainly not suitable interview clothes. This point is shown clearly in a report back from one teacher on the feedback that she received from the headteacher after an unsuccessful interview, where he said that her dress appeared a little short on her, as she was so tall, and she might come across an over-sensitive governor who disapproved.

Now it is not the norm for a headteacher to include a comment on how a candidate dresses in the feedback. If this one did so, it was a warning to the candidate for next time that this dress had probably cost her the job, as it showed poor judgement of what it was appropriate to wear in the context of a school interview. Or indeed of a school.

HORRID PERSONAL HABITS

Poor personal hygiene is the worst offender here. However, I have seen candidates who chew gum throughout the interview, wipe their nose on their sleeve, or males who adjust their clothing (euphemism). Some of the poor manners can be put down to the nerves of the situation. Many candidates will be affected by nerves, although few as badly as the poor young teacher who blurted out to us, as she sat down: *I'm so nervous that I am peeing in my pants*.

Perfect manners, courtesy all the way, is what is required all the time that you are on the premises. I consider that the best way to control your nervousness is to feel that you are well prepared for the interview; you can get this confidence-building preparation by following the advice coming up in this book.

BODY LANGUAGE

L arge tomes have been written on body language and how to use it to your advantage, in interviews and other situations in life. In an interview, I would caution you against trying too hard here, and specifically caution you against the oft-recommended *body language mimic technique*. Firstly it will most probably look contrived, and secondly it will almost certainly distract you from the most important things: listening and responding appropriately.

I suggest that you concentrate on three simple aspects of body language. Firstly, sitting: do not sit on the edge of the chair, all hunched up in defence as though you think that someone is going to come over and punch you. Put a chair in front of the biggest mirror in your house and try sitting like this to see what I mean. Then sit back on the seat of the chair, sit up straight with head up. See the difference? There is normally a table in front of you during an interview, but just in case there isn't, if you are going to be wearing a skirt, check the ride-up factor.

The second point is about eye contact. This can be difficult to do – remember that game you played at primary school as to who could outstare the other? But do try to move your gaze around the panel, making contact first with the person who asks the question, and moving to the others. A tip here is to pretend to make eye contact by fixing your gaze on the bridge of their nose, between their eyes. This will seem like eye contact – try it with a friend across a table.

FACIAL EXPRESSION

T he third point, of course, is that you should smile, even if it is a nervous smile. This can be quite a major issue for some candidates. When doing individual interview coaching with teachers, I have on occasion been supporting clients who seem, on paper, to have everything going for them, yet never make it past the interview. Once we start the mock interview to enable me to evaluate them, it becomes blindingly clear why.

They are, unwittingly, using facial expressions that are extremely off-putting to any observer. I whip out a phone and video them as we continue the interview, and they are horrified as they see themselves apparently glaring at me in extreme annoyance, screwing up their faces while they think, raising their eyes heavenwards in despair, or simply glowering and sending me a furious look. I have had clients who, within thirty seconds of us beginning our mock interview, actually make me feel deeply uncomfortable through the way that they are looking at me.

The only way that you can discover, after a series of unsuccessful interviews, if you have this problem is either to watch yourself (best with a video set up rather than in a mirror), or by getting a friend to give you a mock interview and record it. It could be while holding up your phone, or using Zoom, etc. I talk about this later in the context of video interviews. And then you must learn to smile rather than unwittingly contorting your face into an expression of venom and hatred for the poor panel.

11. THE WRONG SORT OF TALKING

S ome candidates talk themselves out of the job by the wrong sort of talking when faced with the interview panel. There are five things to avoid here, in addition to the obvious error of attempting to crack jokes; even if the person specification included *Good sense of humour*, this is totally inadvisable in any interview.

Talking too fast

Talking too little

Talking too much

Talking too soon

Talking too negatively

TALKING TOO FAST

T alking too fast happens because you are nervous, so you gabble. But the panel needs to hear and understand what you say, so slow down, have brief pauses when you make an important point and look round the panel. If you practice answering questions to the mirror, as I recommend later, try also recording yourself on your phone and then listening critically. If this were a radio programme, would you be impressed with how you come over? Remember that sometimes some members of the panel will not be paying close attention to you, as they will be worrying about how to ask the next question. Keep it calm and unhurried so they do not have to strain to hear you.

TALKING TOO LITTLE

T alking too little is partly because of nerves too; every thought flies out of your head and you come up with a one-word answer. With some candidates, getting them to speak is like attempting to get blood out of a stone.

I can see from your application that you taught years 7 -11 on your teaching practise. Yes.

Have you ever taught the AQA A-level specification? No

I admit that these are not good questions, very bad ones in fact, as they encourage a one-word response; but that's no excuse for answering like that. You should pretend that they said at the end: *Can you tell me briefly about it*, or *Please give a specific example of this.*

Let's do them again:

Have you ever taught the AQA A-level specification?

I saw on your website that that's the one you do, and comparing it with the Edexcel one I'm familiar with, there is a lot of overlap. I liked the different emphasis from AQA that there is in the unit on Child Development, I think that would be very rewarding for the students to study that.

You have given an interesting answer without, incidentally, actually using the word No.

TALKING TOO MUCH

T alking too much – oh please save me from this candidate! It's the person who starts talking before working out what s/he is going to say. Says one thing just to start talking, then thinks: *What shall I say next?* And says it, and then: *What else can I say?* And so it goes on and on and on. Blatantly ignoring all the visual cues from the panel that they wish to say something, and if the chair or the question does attempt to break into this ever-flowing monologue, the candidate just speaks faster and louder in attempt to shout them down. It is not well thought out, it is not planned, it is often only marginally relevant to the question asked. Above all, it takes up the time so that instead of the planned twelve or fifteen questions, we only manage to ask you three or four.

You can often tell if you have been doing that, because when s/he finally manages to get a word in edgeways, the chair will not pass the questioning baton on round the panel, but either say something like: *Steve, I think you've just got one question to ask Anna?*, or go straight into the standard questions at the end. Hoping against hope that you are not going to speak at length when asked if there is anything else that you would like to say in support of your application.

You may feel short-changed on leaving this interview, as you were not asked as many questions as you expected. The truth is that you had the same number of minutes as other candidates, if not more, but just did not make good use of the time.

So you are a rambler; what can you do about it? It is important that you do control it, because this is the main way that candidates talk themselves out of the job. We know that you are nervous, but we are afraid you might be gabbling on like this in class so that children don't get a word in edgeways.

When doing the questions practice that I suggest later on, time yourself. For a complex question, one and a half to two minutes per answer is good, and do make it structured so that it is easy to follow.

Above all, when answering a question, stop and think before opening your mouth. Try to be focussed and organised. Sometimes you can answer with a tight structure, perhaps in three parts. Just briefly, then offering the opportunity to give more.

What do you think are the most important things in keeping children safe in school?

I'd consider three aspects here; health and safety, anti-bullying, and Child Protection procedures. As well as just common sense! Shall I give you an example of something that I would do for one of these?

You could also say: *Would you like me to expand a little here?*

When you are answering a multiple-part question (but not too multiple, please: three or four), it can be helpful both for you and for the panel if you use your fingers and tick off each point. *Health and safety* (tick off one finger), *anti-bullying* (tick off two fingers), and *Child Protection* (tick off a third finger). That gives a visual clue to the panel that you are thinking logically and in an organised fashion.

TALKING TOO SOON

T alking too soon happens when you jump in and start answering a question before the speaker has finished asking it. Just as though you were on University Challenge, jumping in as if you were on a mission to get to the buzzer as fast as possible. Some candidates do just that: they interrupt the interviewer (no Brownie points for that!) and then answer the wrong question.

If you teach secondary subjects, you will be familiar with this answering technique from your students in examinations. A student starts reading the question: *King Lear: discuss the importance of the theme of loyalty*, and thinks: *I know an essay about themes in King Lear!* And then s/he proceeds to regurgitate an essay learnt by heart about the theme of suffering in King Lear.

Something similar can happen in an interview; you hear the beginning of a question, and immediately you think: *That's question 66! That's the 66th of the 100 questions that I wrote out and learnt off!* And you jump in with the answer to the wrong question. Further on I shall give you suggestions of how to prepare intelligently and effectively, how to prepare without learning off by heart tens, scores, hundreds of model answers.

So when you are asked a question, do not jump in too fast, but pause and think. Ask for clarification if necessary, and do not hesitate to repeat the question to be sure that you have grasped it, especially if it is in several parts. Here's an example:

How do you relate to pupils in their mid-teens? Can you adopt their mannerisms and slang, do you treat them as peers and share their humour?

At this point, repeating, re-wording the question enables you to ensure that you have understood it, as well as giving you some thinking time.

So, relating to the older pupils, adopting the same sort of speech and mannerisms, sharing a teen-humour joke with them . . .

So, here's a challenge for you: how are you going to answer this question? Think it through before reading on to see what I have to say.

No, I do not. This is not the way to establish an effective professional relationship with pupils. I'm the teacher, I am expected to be a role model and act objectively in the best interests of the pupils. I shouldn't model my behaviour on the pupils' behaviour, following their lead.

So I relate to them professionally, with mutual respect but not as peers, as I am not their peer, I am their teacher.

N.B. – this question is an actual example from some of the Child Protection training for interviewers, and that is the model answer that was given. So it is a question with a correct answer! I talk later about preparing this topic.

TALKING TOO NEGATIVELY

This is the final example of the wrong talking. There is a simple solution to this: never say anything negative about your current or past employers or schools, nor about your training. Of course you are unlikely to answer this way:

So what was your PGCE course like at St Hildegard's College?

Awful! It was just awful! The lecturers weren't at all helpful, their seminars were just downloaded from the internet, they never marked any essays, and they were totally useless at giving you any tips on how to manage in TP. I wish I'd never gone there.

If your training was that bad, then you are not well trained, possibly incompetent, so why should I appoint you? This answer is clearly a poor one, as nobody wants as a teacher somebody who is incompetent. But avoid all other negative comments, as nobody wants a moaner, nobody wants somebody who might go on to be indiscreet about their school, nobody wants somebody who is trying to get away from their current school rather than wanting specifically to come to your school.

That last point is important. Schools are looking for pilgrims, teachers who are hoping to make the journey to that particular school because of what it is and what it does. They do not want refugees, fleeing from their current position and prepared to go just anywhere as long as they get away. ***Pilgrims not refugees***; remember that.

A further point to realise is that talking negatively can come out almost subconsciously, especially through the use of the word *unfortunately*. Avoid using that at all costs; train yourself not to say it.

What experience do you have of doing fieldwork with GCSE pupils?

Unfortunately, I couldn't go on the fieldwork trip last year because I was ill.

Do you like being a Form Tutor? Which year group would you prefer?

Unfortunately . . .

(It doesn't matter what you say next – the panel has already heard that forbidden word).

Let's have another go at this, putting the positive not negative side forward.

What experience do you have of doing fieldwork with GCSE pupils?

I am really looking forward to that experience with my pupils! Last year I helped with the organisation beforehand, and of course with the curriculum preparation and then the follow-up work based on it. This year I shall be in there wearing my wellingtons!

Just one thing to add here; if you are asked something and do not know what to answer, just say so. Briefly and politely, but do not go scrambling around for an answer if you know perfectly well that you have no idea. One failure to respond should not be held against you if the rest is top notch.

12. THE WRONG SORT OF PREPARATION

My main advice to any candidate before any interview is always three don'ts.

- Don't research websites; they will be too American and too business-orientated
- Don't rely on interview guidance books, many of which also are American
- And above all, do not learn answers to questions off by heart.

These are the lazy and ineffective ways of preparing for an interview.

13. THE RIGHT SORT OF PREPARATION

The intelligent and effective way to prepare is to have prepared the topic areas, a thematic preparation, rather than just standard answers learnt by heart that you then recite like a Dalek.

There are two stages here to this preparation: identifying the areas to prepare, and then how to prepare them.

THE TOPICS FOR PREPARATION

Which are the topics likely to be discussed in the interview? Since the interview is to explore to what extent you meet the criteria set out in the person specification and job description for one specific school, then these, and not some book or website of 100 interview questions and answers for teachers, should be your starting point. These topics are, of course, the ones that are part of the ES (executive summary) that you probably submitted with your application, because they are the topics specifically identified by the school in their documentation sent out to applicants.

There are three other areas that form topics to prepare. The first two are the school's BBs (buying buttons) and your USPs (unique selling points). More in a moment about these acronyms. You could also look at the *Teachers' Standards*, or if more appropriate, the *Headteachers' Standards (2020)*, and use their headers for your preparation too. Of course Safeguarding, Child Protection and Prevent should also be prepared.

It sounds like an awful lot to prepare, but it is less than you think, after the first interview, which will indeed involve a great deal of preparation. This is why I suggest that you begin it as soon as you have sent off your application. Let's consider the four areas of preparation:

The ES – many of these elements will be similar in different schools

Their BBs – there will be some overlap between different schools as some BBs are constant

Your USPs – these are likely to be almost exactly the same, unless you are applying for wildly differing schools, and choose not to tell the school in rural Devon about your experience in multi-cultural Lambeth

The standards – once this preparation is done, it's done for ever. However, this is the one that you might consider not doing, if pushed for time

Safeguarding, Child Protection and Prevent – a clear one-off but essential

At this point I will give you another extract from the document I have quoted before: **Keeping children safe in education 2022 Statutory guidance for schools and colleges, 1 September 2022.**

The interviews should be used to explore potential areas of concern and to determine the applicant's suitability to work with children. Areas that may be concerning and lead to further probing include:

• implication that adults and children are equal

• lack of recognition and/or understanding of the vulnerability of children

• inappropriate idealisation of children

• inadequate understanding of appropriate boundaries between adults and children, and,

• indicators of negative safeguarding behaviours.

Any information about past disciplinary action or substantiated allegations should be considered in the circumstances of the individual case.

You should ensure that you bear the above in mind when preparing this important topic.

I am now going to summarise briefly part of the sections of the previous book **Applying for a Teaching Job 2022-3**, to remind you about the ES, the BBs and the USPs. If you need a fuller reminder, and to see again the examples given, you will need to go back and re-read it.

An executive summary is a two-column table. In the left-hand column are their criteria for appointment, and in the right-hand one, your evidence in brief note form that you meet their requirements. Its aim is to do their task of shortlisting for them, because that generally is how we shortlist candidates.

The normal procedure for shortlisting is that we draw up a large table with the criteria in the left-hand column, then a number of columns, one for each applicant, where we go down putting a tick or cross next to each criterion, finally putting a Y or a N at the very bottom of each column for whether we wish to invite them in for an interview. The executive summary replicates this structure of criterion + evidence. One very important point about an executive summary is that it must have appropriate and strong evidence as your proof of meeting a criterion, otherwise it is only emphasising your ineptitude.

How, therefore, do you draw up an executive summary for a job application? You start by examining the school's person specification, noting which criteria are essentials and which only desirables; unless you have something extra-special under the desirable heading, you can usually omit all those points. It may also be appropriate to use some of the job description, including tasks that you already carry out well.

You will omit a criterion for which you have no evidence; if it asks for "*At least three years' experience teaching GCSE*" and you have only two, don't include that in the summary where your failure to meet that requirement will attract their attention.

And since they do not ask for this summary, why should you do it? Because it does their shortlisting for them, showing them exactly how you tick their boxes for selection for interview.

An HR professional in a large Academy chain said:

The summary sets out clearly the applicant's skills and experience, and matches it exactly to what we are looking for, enabling the selection committee to shortlist fairly and impartially by our stated criteria.

Identify the school's buying buttons. You may have already done this for your application statement or letter. What is a buying button? It is used in sales to identify what it is that the customer is looking for, so that when you press that button by mentioning this feature of the product, they want to buy. Different people – and different schools – may have different buying buttons. A salesperson wishing to sell double-glazing to one person would push the BB of: *You will save on heating costs*. For another potential customer, the BB might be: *Won't the neighbours be impressed by your smart new windows!*

Find out what it is that the school wants for its pupils by reading all its paperwork and scrutinising its website and, if it has one, prospectus. What is it that the school is looking for? What are its values? What is really important to them? What can you do to help achieve this? An obvious buying button for most schools is learning and progress for all, but schools will word this differently (check their website), and have other aspects that are important to them.

Know yourself and your USPs Remember, it's all about the pupils and what you specifically can offer them. You need to define fully your USPs. Hopefully, you have done some work already on this for your application statement or letter.

If not, then now identify three (or possibly four) USPs. They have to be about you, not USPs that someone else has suggested, because they have to want you, because it's you who is going to have to do the job, fit in with the rest of the school, etc, so giving them answers that do not show you but someone else is just not sensible.

So think of your USPs; here some examples of draft USPs, just to give you a general idea. They are not all perfectly worded yet – you do not have to get them right first time round, you do a first draft then polish them a bit so they are just right.

I have good communication skills with parents

I am very committed to the pastoral side of working with pupils

I am prepared to work very hard for the children

I am very analytical and clear-headed

I am very caring about the whole child

I think academic success for all students must be our aim

I enjoy working cooperatively for materials preparation

This is too many, of course, and anyway you should not copy any of these because it is very unlikely that they will be exactly who and what you are.

It is very hard to think of your USPs; it almost seems like boasting, on the one hand, and on the other you are probably not used to doing this kind of self-analysis. But do persevere as it is very important to have these clearly in your mind.

Here are my USPs, me, Theo Griff:

Committed and hard-working

High levels of analytical intelligence, you can't pull the wool over my eyes

* Passionate about children, their welfare, their education and their success

This is me now, not as a school leader but as an education consultant. If I were still a school leader, I would have different USPs to give. If I were still a teacher, my USPs would be different again, because I would be at a different stage in my career, but also because out of a slightly larger number of USPs, all of them honest and truthful about me, I would select the most appropriate ones for this specific application.

An important point about your USPs is that they should match the school's BBs – their buying buttons, what it is that they are looking for, what they need for this specific post; you may need to choose between some of your USPs to fit a specific school.

Be careful to identify what are the school's BBs and check the USPs that you choose to discuss in the interview, to ensure that there is a good overlap. And, of course, although you should read carefully their documentation and website, remember that there are hidden BBs, or at least BBs that are taken for granted. Standard BBs might be *Raising achievement, The whole child, The Catholic ethos,* etc.

THE METHODS FOR PREPARATION

Having determined which are the topic areas to prepare for the interview, you now set yourself up with either pencil and paper, or an appropriate computer programme, for doing mind maps. Hopefully you are already well acquainted with this technique and know already which you prefer – hand drawn, or computer generated.

If you are a newcomer to this technique, there are lots of websites and books to help you with mind mapping, and also several short videos on YouTube that explain the principles and give examples.

Your mind maps will always be work in progress. Start off with one topic – perhaps classroom management – and do the first few ideas that come to you. Then pick another topic, one of your USPs, for example, and work for a few minutes on that too. Keep moving on to another topic – you will often find that this means that something pops into your mind for an earlier topic, so go back to it and add it. Keep building these up over several days, adding examples of your own experience when you have sufficient idea bubbles.

Having developed a mind map to a certain stage, when it is more than just two or three bubbles, start looking at it and talking to it, explaining out loud (that is very important) explaining out loud what it means, expanding on the short notes you've written. Try closing your eyes and visualising it, saying out loud what the different elements are. Then try it again with your eyes open, as though you were talking about it in the staffroom to a colleague.

This will get you used to talking about the topics spontaneously, naturally, thinking of a topic and then pulling out your image of the bubbles so you can talk about them without just pushing out a pre-digested pre-learnt answer.

This is intelligent preparation, the sort of preparation that will enable you to impress at interview in a way that no learnt-by-heart answers from a book will.

THE BEST QUESTION TO BE ASKED AT AN INTERVIEW

T he dream question, from the point of view of a candidate, is one that many of you fear. It can be worded in a number of ways, the most common being quite simply: *Tell us about yourself.*

What should you say? It's easier first to say what you should not say, which is that you should not give a potted biography:

I was brought up at first in Wales, then moved to Bristol where I was a pupil at Colston's Girls' School before going to the University of Exeter where I studied History. Then I did my PGCE and got my first job in . . .

You might just as well tell them your shoe size, height and weight, for all the good that sort of information would do you in getting this job. I have read a number of other very unhelpful suggestions in interview books or on websites as to how you should answer this question. Here is one example:

Try starting out by sharing some personal interests which do not relate directly to your work. Examples might include a hobby which you are passionate about like quilting, astronomy, chess, choral singing, golf, skiing, tennis, or antiquing.

Interests like long distance running or yoga which help to represent your healthy, energetic side are worth mentioning. Pursuits like being an avid reader or solving crossword puzzles or brain teasers will help to showcase your intellectual leaning. Interests like golf, tennis, and gourmet food might have some value if you would be entertaining clients in your new job.

Volunteer work will demonstrate the seriousness of your character and commitment to the welfare of your community.

Interactive roles like PTA volunteer, museum tour guide, fundraiser, or chair of a social club will help show your comfort with engaging others.

I make that six different things that you should talk about: hobby, healthy activity, intellectual activity, client entertainment, character and commitment and finally the topic of engaging with others. The poor panel won't know what's hit them. That example is clearly not for teaching – you don't often have the opportunity to entertain clients in Key Stage 3 – but giving all this personal information would just take up too much time on items that are not going to help demonstrate that you would be an effective teacher in this school.

The next extract I really enjoyed reading – in fact I enjoyed the whole of its advice for UK teacher interviews. Not only because it is so false sounding, but also because it is so obviously somebody writing in the States but believing that UK teachers would find this useful if it were just made relevant to them by throwing in a few UK references:

I am a confident, enthusiastic person with a genuine passion and desire for improving the education of young people. I myself have a great education, and achieved high GCSE grades, A-levels, undergrad and postgrad marks in my subject field – English. I recently completed my PGCE teacher training and am now ready to move into the world of work.

It is, I realise, not appropriate to insert a smiley into a book, but I am tempted, I am very tempted, at this point.

Instead of any of these inept answers above, at this point you bring out your USPs, carefully worded to ensure that they meet some of the school's BBs, and you say:

There are three main things I'd like to tell you about myself. Firstly X, secondly Y, and then Z. Would you like me to give you an example for one of these?

Obviously X,Y and Z are your three USPs. The example that you give will come from your mind map of the USPs. You have now done the equivalent of a 30-second advertisement at half time in the Cup Final on television. It is an advertisement that is selling you, setting out clearly your strengths and why you are right for this specific job in this specific school. Moreover, you have placed this advertisement right at the beginning of the interview, as this is an opener-type question. This should make you feel good and give you confidence for the rest of the interview, as well as giving the panel a favourable impression of you right from the start.

Another very common question is: *Why have you applied for this post?* This can often also be worded as: *What motivated you to apply for this post?* Or again: *Why does this post interest you?* And, unfortunately, a very common answer is how it is all to your advantage to be appointed.

In my long experience, people actually **do** say that they are applying because the school is convenient for dropping off their children. But even more common are teachers who say things like: *Because it would help me develop my management skills in a new context,* or: *It would provide the ideal environment for my NQT year,* or: *It would be a new challenge that I would relish.*

Apart from suggesting that you never let the word *challenge* pass your lips during an interview (unless referring to challenges for students), my advice here is to consider carefully; *is this appointment supposed to be to your advantage, or to the panel's?*

To be blunt, a panel is not in the least interested in the advantages to you of this post; they are interested only in the advantages for them of appointing you. But with intelligent preparation, this is another dream question, enabling you to get over clearly and succinctly to the panel how it is in their interest to appoint you.

Think now of what you would do for them if appointed.

I have applied for this post because I believe that I can contribute to A, B and C.

A, B and C are, of course, slightly differently-worded versions of your USPs. You could have similar questions, such as: *What could you bring to this school? Why should we appoint you?* So it is a good idea to have several versions of your USPs (not saying completely different things about you – you can't suddenly change who you are, but slight variations, and differently worded) that you can use in slightly different contexts.

Including at the end, when you are asked, with any luck: *Is there anything else that you would like to say in support of your application?* This is your last chance to show them, clearly and succinctly, why they should appoint you.

I would just like to reiterate what I said earlier, that I can bring to this school X, Y and Z, which would benefit your pupils and your school overall by . . .

That would be an ideal closing statement to an interview.

14. PUTTING THE PREPARATION INTO PRACTICE

I t's all very well you sitting there reading what I've written, but the way to develop expertise in a particular skill or technique is to practise it. The more you practise, and the more regularly that you practice, the better you get. So this is the next step.

And this is also why you should start your interview preparation well in advance of being invited to interview. Start the preparation, all of it, the moment you have sent off your application.

Start by inventing some questions based on the mind maps that you have done from their person specification and job description, plus from the Standards, and from Child protection, Safeguarding and Prevent. You can also get some more questions from the internet – make sure that they are UK questions, however. Add: *What could you bring to this school? Why should we appoint you? Why have you applied for this post? What motivated you to apply for this post? Tell us about yourself. Is there anything else that you would like to say in support of your application?* Organise them into categories: introduction, general, theory and philosophy of teaching, curriculum, behaviour, parents, teamwork, or whatever suits you best.

Print out two sets. One set you keep for whoever will be obliging enough to give you a mock interview, the other you cut into little strips, one question per strip. These little strips you put into a carrier bag or old A4 envelope.

Sit yourself on a chair in front of a large mirror, preferably full length. This is probably in a bedroom, hopefully yours rather than that of your teenage daughter. If there is anyone else in the house, close the door.

Sit up straight, smile at yourself – the mirror image is the panel - put your hand in the bag or envelope and pull out a strip. Read it out aloud, pause briefly to think, then smiling in the mirror, answer aloud the question. The aloud part is important – you need to get used to hearing the questions out loud, then speaking your answers out loud, while smiling as appropriate, rather than just going through them in your head. The smiling bit is important, don't forget it.

You can try recording a few answers, and also timing them from the recording, to check the speed of your delivery (How did you sound? Were you gabbling nineteen to the dozen? Were you leaving too-long pauses?) and the length of an answer – one and a half to two minutes for a well-structured reply is ample.

When you pull out a question, think of your mind maps – visualise what is around it on the map. Ask also if one of their BBs or your USPs can be brought casually into the answer. You must always know where you are going with your answer before you shoot off into the unknown, just talking for the sake of talking. Wherever possible, make your answers structured, perhaps ticking off the different sections on your fingers as I suggested.

Do this every single day for 20 – 30 minutes, from as soon as you have organised your preparation until the actual day of the interview. Speaking aloud, hearing a question and relating it to your mind maps, practising, practising, practising.

You also need to do at least one mock interview with someone who is prepared not to pull the punches; your line manager at school would be an excellent choice, but so would a bossy sibling or partner.

Dress up smartly as for an interview (but not your actual interview outfit which must be kept pristine); this will ensure that you feel slightly stressed and uncomfortable before you have even begun. Give them the list of questions and tell them to pick their own choice from each section. If it is someone who can tell you if your answers are plain rubbish, so much the better. But at the very least you will get feedback on how you come over, any irritating habits such as twisting your ring or fiddling with your moustache, whether you are just going on and on and on in an answer with no logical structure, and whether you are smiling or glaring at the interviewer.

If you are going to have a video interview, then a mock interview using the same technology would be good, so set up Zoom or Meet or whatever on two computers and record it, of course.

15. THE WRONG QUESTIONS AT THE END

There is usually an opportunity to ask questions at the end. I always ask if there are any urgent questions, not just any questions, to try to prevent candidates from making the mistake here of asking just any old question. Because at this stage, you should not have any questions which either haven't already been answered from the documentation or from being in school, or are of relatively little importance anyway.

Please be aware that this is an information opportunity, not an opportunity for you to show off your preparedness by bringing out a list of questions.

There is really only one sort of question that you should ask, although hopefully even that one has been answered already, so in most cases you can reply:

Thank you, I have been able to find out everything that I need to about the school already - your colleague was very helpful as we walked around the premises.

At the end of the interview, you ask only those questions that you need to know to enable you to decide whether or not to accept the post, were it to be offered, and in exceptional circumstances only. There are people who lose the interview for themselves at this point, by asking a trivial question, something that was explained in the documentation or on the website, or by asking a question to impress.

I myself and other headteachers have the experience of more than one candidate taking out a whole list of questions, a whole list, (including the fabulously trivial *"Will I get a locker in the staffroom?"*) and reading methodically through it. If you try, politely, to bring things to a close, you may be greeted with a plaintive : *"But I was told it was important to show an interest by having questions to ask!".*

This unnecessary question-asking just annoys the panel who have a timetable to keep with the next candidate sitting waiting.

One sort of essential question that I would consider totally acceptable for a candidate to ask would be:

I am an Orthodox Jew - would it be possible for the timetable to be arranged so that my PPA is late on Friday afternoons, to allow me to travel home before sunset in winter for Shabbat?

The other sort of question is one that you should not need to ask, but may have to, if the school has neglected to make this clear. Now that there is no automatic recognition of the pay you earned in one school when you go to the next (that's called pay portability), you may well need to bring up the question of how much they will pay you. You can word it thus:

In the event of my being your preferred candidate, may I raise the delicate subject of salary? Have you made a decision about what my pay level would be; does your pay policy recognise pay portability from my current post?

You should avoid asking any other questions, especially questions to impress us or foil us. Questions about Ofsted normally fall into both these categories. The very worst kind of questions to ask is just that: something that turns the tables, that starts interviewing the interviewers, in an apparent attempt to show how superior the candidate is. People often think that this shows them off as being on-the-ball and will impress the panel. No, it does not.

Since the time when on-line teaching was the norm, what has the school been doing to combat the negative impact on teaching and learning, and on teacher and pupil welfare?

Another horrible example is this sort of thing:

How have you raised standards and improved attendance since your last Ofsted Report?

And I was once asked by an (unsuccessful) applicant for a deputy headteacher post:

I have seen your Five-year Strategic Plan. Could you please tell me what your strategic objectives are for ten years' time?

And again, take care with questions suggested by your university tutor:

Can you tell me how you are implementing the X policy? Or the one which makes me wonder if you are going to do catch-up learning on your own: *What was the subject of your last staff Inset?*

Equally inappropriate are the questions put forward by some of the interview books and websites:

Could you use a teacher like me in your school?

Is there anything else I need to do to convince you that I am the person to appoint?

No question is best here.

16. FINALLY

FINAL IMPRESSIONS

T here are two questions that are often asked at the end:

If offered, would you accept this post? Sometimes worded as:

Are you still interested in this post?

You are being put on the spot here. Really the only answer is: *Yes.* But if you haven't just answered about additional information in support of your application, you could possibly expand this answer just a little, using some positive points, possibly linked to their BBs, to show that you understand the school ethos:

Yes, I believe that I have a lot to contribute to the school and would like to work with a team of teachers who . . .

Do not bother to say *"Subject to contract"* or *"Subject to appropriate pay and conditions"*; you'll just sound daft putting in a semi-legal phrase when this is not in any way something that could be considered a legal or contractual commitment.

FINAL WARNING

Do please remember that the interview has only ended when you are off school premises and out of sight. Do not immediately light up a cigarette as soon as you are in the playground, nor make some carefree and careless meant-to-be-humorous remark to a group of students, just because you are feeling relieved. Remember that you are still on show, still under interview conditions.

Once I was courteously escorting a candidate back to reception after her interview, when she asked me: *"Is that it, now?"* *"Yes"*, I reassured her. *"We are just going to collect your travel claim form"*. *"Oh thank goodness! I was scared you'd ask me about what happened last summer on the student history visit to Germany."*

You can imagine what I said next, in a sympathetic tone: *"Oh dear, that does sound upsetting. What was it that happened?"* She explained how she and several sixth-formers had been arrested for the German equivalent of being drunk and disorderly.

17. AFTER THE INTERVIEW

You should review your performance by writing down as soon as possible the questions that they asked you, even in the bus or train if you came that way, before you forget. Review the interview overall, what went well, what less well in your view. How could you improve next time? How good were your answers, could you have made them better by using one of the techniques above more effectively?

Do this straight away, before you receive the telephone call, so that it is not overshadowed by hearing the result. You may indeed have performed very well, answered coherently and in a structured fashion, showed yourself to be thoroughly professional and very appointable, yet still not got the job because another candidate had something extra to offer.

HOW IS IT DECIDED WHOM TO APPOINT?

The decision on who to appoint is made by the panel. I think that it is important that everyone understands this. We are very grateful for the contribution of others – anyone who did the observations if not on the panel, the student council, the department staff who met the candidates; but it is the panel that makes the decision. You sometimes have a department who consider that their coffee meet is when the decision is made, and say: *We want So-and-so to be appointed.* No. The decision is the panel's.

And within the panel, it is the chair who has the casting vote if needed. This means the headteacher, or the chair of governors, or the CEO of the academy trust. They are the ones with whom the ultimate responsibility lies for the quality of learning and teaching in the school.

So how does the panel decide? Every interviewing panel is different, of course, but we all want the absolute best teacher for our school. When I am chairing the panel, I remind everybody of that, and add that if that best teacher isn't here today, then we re-advertise.

We have a person specification (what sort of person and what sort of teacher that we want the successful candidate to be, their skills and experience) and a job description (what they will have to do). We try to measure the candidates up against these, to answer the three questions that we are asking ourselves:

Can these candidates do the job, do they have the right skills and experience?

Will they do the job, do they have the right attitude, the commitment?

And finally, will they do the job in the way that we want it done, following our ethos?

Of course, we also explore their suitability to work with children, as set out above in the extract from **Keeping children safe in education 2022 Statutory guidance for schools and colleges**; this is a very important consideration.

We request your references before the interview, to allow us to ask you in the interview about any concerns, or even to query any discrepancies between your application and the references:

You speak in your application about your excellent results at GCSE with your last two groups. But the headteacher says that they were disappointing as you had the top sets and they did no better than the middle sets, and you achieved lower value-added; can you therefore just outline for us why you consider these results to be outstanding?

During the interview, we take notes. Often we have a score sheet where we score one or more aspects of each answer (fluency, knowledge of theory, etc) – scoring out of 5 is quite common – as well as having brief notes too. We can then add up these scores to help us clarify our views.

We then weigh up all the evidence to decide who is the best candidate. The applications, the references, your classes' results, the teaching or other task, the performance in interview, the overall impression that we have formed of you, including the all-important first impression when you walked into the interview room, and our judgment on how you would fit in with the rest of the team, balancing their strengths with yours.

I said that we then weigh up all the evidence to decide who is the best candidate, but often we begin by identify any candidate who is felt by the whole panel to be unsuitable for appointment. So we will start by eliminating carefully, listening to the comments made by each member in favour of or against each person. One or two unanimous *No's* will clear the decks before we consider the top-performing candidates and try to differentiate between them. We try at all times to be fair, and to make judgments that are not only based on clear evidence but also do not discriminate against any class of candidate.

But sometimes there are several very good, even outstanding, candidates, all with the same scores on our score sheets, all with the same number of positive aspects to their teaching, all who performed well at interview. But there is one of these who just clicks with us. I think it's a bit like falling in love – you know you're in love, but you can't quite explain why. And that, sometimes, is how we decide who we're going to appoint.

THE TELEPHONE CALL

You will normally have been asked to give a phone number where you can be contacted that evening, and a time when you would be available. If possible, do not be picky over the time, and do not go out to the pub thinking you can take the call on your mobile. It would be too noisy there.

Even if they have been unable to make the decision, the school should still call you when they said that they would, if only to say that they will be unable to give you the decision until tomorrow.

You can normally tell from the tone of voice whether it's good news. You might even be able to tell by who is ringing; I always let the line manager give the good news, and once we had an accepted offer, I would ring the unsuccessful candidates with the bad news. This allowed one of the first contacts between the new colleague and the line manager to be a very positive experience, and gave me the less palatable task of disappointing the other candidates.

Have a pen and paper handy. If the news is good, first thank them, accept, and say that you look forward to joining the school and making a positive contribution. Then ask for confirmation of the title, the salary and the starting date, and whether the post is full time and permanent or not. Write it all down, read it all back to the person who rang so that you are completely in agreement about what has been said. Ask when you will be receiving confirmation in writing, as you would not wish to withdraw from other interviews without this.

Thank them again and then, only then, open a bottle; you do not wish to take the call offering the job after you have already downed half a bottle of Sauvignon.

Sometimes they do not ring when they said that they would; not to let you know the result when you have been interviewed is discourteous, or at the very least poor organisation, with some lack of clarity about who is in charge of this task.

If at the interview they say that they will ring that evening, then they should. They may have to ring to say that there is no decision yet, so they will ring tomorrow. But ring you that evening they really should. Of course, sometimes they have not yet decided, for one reason or another. It may be that they are unsure, as there are two seemingly equal candidates. Perhaps even there has been an emergency; the headteacher's partner is in an accident, so that they cannot even begin discussing the decision. These things can happen.

Sometimes they cannot actually tell you if you have the job or not, because the first-choice candidate is inconveniently unavailable, or has asked for 24 hours to think about it. They will not wish to tell you yet that you were unsuccessful, in case they have to turn to you as Plan B. They will say, therefore, that the panel hasn't yet finished its deliberations, because they would rather that you didn't know that you were second choice, when they finally get round to offering you. This delay, however, should not prevent them from ringing the candidates to say that there will be no announcement just yet of the decision.

DRAFT A FIRST ACCEPTANCE

If the telephone call brings the news that you have been offered the job, and you accept it, then draft an e-mail something like this shown below. No need to put the date at the top, as an e-mail is already dated automatically.

Dear Dr Griffiths

Full-time permanent post of teacher of Spanish and French

I am writing to confirm my acceptance of the offer made to me on the telephone by Mrs Sharpes, head of modern foreign languages, on the evening of Thursday 12 May.

She offered and I accepted during that conversation the full-time permanent post of teacher of Spanish and French at Greengates Academy, beginning on 1st September 2022, at a starting salary of £34,502.

On receiving written confirmation of this offer, I shall withdraw from all other applications.

I would be pleased to receive also any other paperwork that I should fill in and return to you prior to the beginning of my employment.

I look forward to joining my new colleagues and contributing to the continuing success of Greengates Academy.

Yours sincerely,

William Beaumont

Their telephone offer and your acceptance have contractual force, but obviously, a verbal offer and acceptance have as their major disadvantage a lack of proof. By sending this e-mail off quickly, it gives an evidence trail. Make it formal, and amend it to suit the offer that was made; be careful to include full-time permanent if that was what the job was, and that was what you were offered. Of course, you should not accept a full-time permanent post if it was a fixed-term one, or a part-time position.

If it is part time, then say the agreed percentage:

She offered and I accepted during that conversation the permanent part-time (0.75) post of teacher of Spanish and French at Greengates Academy, beginning on 1st September 2022, at a starting salary of £34,502 pro-rata.

If you have got this wrong, and, for example, they offered not a permanent post but a fixed-term one, they should get back to you quickly to say so.

It is always good to get these details correct right from the start. When they write a letter with the offer, write back, a letter this time, thanking them and accepting again. You should also start a file folder with all the school's paperwork.

ASKING FOR FEEDBACK

Interview feedback quite often does not seem to make sense. The school agrees to provide feedback as to why you were not appointed, and then says that it was because of your lack of experience, or the fact that you could only teach one science at KS4, or some other thing that was already very clear from your application. They already knew that, so why did they even shortlist you?

The trouble with giving feedback is that the school often does not know what to say to the unsuccessful candidates, for several reasons. Firstly, they are worried that their feedback might offend; I have to hang my head with shame here and say that I have failed to give honest feedback to the candidates with poor personal hygiene, despite having to suspend the interviews for 15 minutes in order to air the room after they left.

They may also be concerned that their feedback might bite back at them, that they might receive a letter from your solicitor saying:

My client informs me that your justification for non-appointment was X. However, since in fact she does have X, Y and Z, there is clearly a covert reason, which we believe to be gender discrimination. We are therefore. . .

A further reason may be that an appointment committee

cannot put into words why they chose A and not B. On paper they both looked good, in the lesson they both did well, and on the interview score sheet, conscientiously filled in by all the panel, they came out with equal scores. But somehow, in the interview, A just seemed to click with them, to develop a relationship which made them feel that s/he would be a valued colleague.

I said above that on occasion, appointing a candidate is a bit like falling in love. You know that you are in love, you know that you do love him or her, but you cannot explain why.

So for all those reasons (do you really want to be told that they just liked the successful candidate more?), schools tend to go for the bland feedback: (*you were pipped at the post*), the easy feedback: (*if we had had two posts we would have appointed you*), and the safe, cannot be disproven feedback: (*we appointed somebody with more/less experience*).

The feedback experience can be even worse if you receive contradictory feedback from two schools; one says that your answers were too brief, the other that your answers were too rambling, and since you hadn't received the first feedback before the second interview, and felt that you answered in pretty similar ways, you are now confused about how to improve for next time.

So is it worth even asking for feedback? I have always declined to give instant feedback after an interview. With the rest of the panel, we think of one positive to tell the unsuccessful candidate when we give the bad news:

I'm afraid that this is not the news that you were hoping for. We particularly liked your good classroom management, but have decided to offer the post to another candidate.

We then offer to discuss this later on, saying that it is not our policy to offer feedback immediately, as we know that candidates may be too disappointed to take it all in now. If they would like to ring back in a week and speak to the headteacher's secretary, they will get an appointment for receiving some suggestions for any future applications.

The headteacher's secretary, because it is also my policy that the person who gets paid the most deals with the people who are going to be most unhappy when they get the bad news.

So my suggestion to you is that you e-mail the school in a week's time. Do not ask for feedback, but ask instead if they could give you a time when someone could pass on some positive suggestions about how you could improve your application and interview next time. Asking for feedback might make them feel uncomfortable, as it could be seen as asking them to criticise you. But asking for suggestions to improve, asking for positives - they will feel better about that.

18. INTERNAL INTERVIEWS AND INTERNAL CANDIDATES

If you are an internal candidate, there may be moments in the interview when you feel uncomfortable. When some passing year 8 girl calls out: *Sir! Sir! Are you on interview?*, and the other candidates turn towards you with a look of horror, as you are the dreaded internal candidate who is rumoured to be always the favoured one. Or at the *meet the colleagues* coffee break, when your own colleagues, i.e. everyone there, ignore you to get to know the other candidates.

The school should do their best to ensure that you get the same treatment as the other candidates on interview day. That means, for example, that you go on the group school tour if there is one, and especially that you are not expected to do cloakroom duty, or teach a class, in any pauses in the schedule. You should also have the same questions in the interview, and teach a class that you do not normally teach nor have taught in the past. You should play the game too, and not nip off to have a chat with some friend, nor take advantage of your familiarity with the stationery cupboard.

As an internal applicant, you have the advantage of knowing the school. But this over-familiarity has its downside. You may think that you do not need to prepare as well as the other candidates – oh yes you do – and in particular you may think that you do not need to tell the panel everything, that since they already know all that you do, it would in fact be daft to tell them everything. Oh yes you do need to tell them. *Everything*.

In both your application and your interview, you should act as though you were applying to another school where they do not know you at all. You need to spell out everything exactly as you would in an unknown context. The panel needs to have a similar picture of you, your values, skills, and experience as they do of the other candidates, so that they can weigh you all up. Since most panels score answers on a score sheet to help in their decision-making, what you do not say, what you do not tell them, you can get no credit for, and thus no score. Where internal candidates tend to fail, it is due to underselling themselves.

INTERNAL CANDIDATES ALWAYS GET THE JOB

I t is a well-known fact, well known that is to anyone who has not been appointed when an internal candidate was, that internal candidates always get the job. The same teachers, probably, who say that some people are only at the interview to make up the numbers and that it has already been decided beforehand who is going to be appointed.

As a well-known interviewer, I actually take exception to both of these assertions. My response is: *How do you know? How often have you been part of a selection panel for teaching posts in a school? Not very often? So from where do you get this insider information?*

Schools go to a lot of time and effort organising and running lessons observations and interviews. We don't just give the jobs to internal candidates as a gift, even though we could do so without going to the expense, time and trouble of interviewing at all – there is no law that says we must advertise and conduct formal interviews at all, you see. We don't bring in extra candidates who are no-hopers just to make up the numbers, because that means more time and effort for us. More importantly, we don't do it because we wish to be fair and honest in our appointment procedures.

Internal candidates sometimes get the job, and sometimes they do not. It's just that it is noticed more when they are successful than when they are not appointed. I myself have lost out to internal candidates, and also I have been appointed when there have been two internal candidates.

I will tell you something else about internal candidates. Sometimes they are shortlisted because the headteacher is weak. Instead of calling in the internal candidate and telling him or her that they haven't been shortlisted, this is why they were not selected, and this is how the school is proposing giving the experience that they are missing, they shortlist them even though they are not of the same calibre as the other candidates. Then when they fail to be appointed, the blame becomes corporate: *the panel didn't wish to appoint you, I'm afraid.*

So if you are an internal candidate, remember my advice above about solid preparation and ensuring that you sell yourself. If you are an external candidate, do not fear the internal; s/he may or may not get the job, just as you may or may not.

19. INTERVIEWS FOR INDEPENDENT SCHOOLS

T hese interviews can on some occasions be more formal than for other schools, with a larger interview panel, and also a lot less formal or even slightly unconventional or downright weird on other occasions; I have heard of interviews where the headteacher had his dog in the room and candidates were invited to greet the canine companion who, they were told, would be playing a part in the selection. What is not too uncommon in independent schools is that part of the interview schedule includes an interview with the candidate alone with the headteacher. With or without a pet.

My comments about independent school interviews would be firstly that you should pay especial notice to appearance - suits are appreciated, tattoos are not - and secondly that you should be ready to talk about how you could contribute to the co-curricular life of the school. Look on the website and see the full range of sports and activities that they offer. Could you help run one of these? Is there any other interest of yours that could be the basis of a new activity to offer? Be prepared also to talk about how you would cope with demanding parents, with examples ready to hand from your mind map.

The other area where you need to take care is in the

observed lesson. If you currently teach outside the independent sector, you may be surprised at the level of classroom behaviour; in general you will not, here, waste time settling the class down, as the following tale shows.

Some years ago when I was doing Ofsted training, one of my fellow trainees, a head of department from a comprehensive school, visited my independent school for the day. We were walking around when we came to a year 9 classroom with the door open; we looked in. The class was working from textbooks in almost complete silence, heads down, just the odd murmur. There was no teacher in sight, and I enquired what lesson it was and why there was no teacher. A pupil spoke up to say that the teacher hadn't come, so the form captain had told everybody to get out their maths book and go on with the next exercises until the teacher turned up; which they were still doing, 20 minutes into the lesson.

My colleague said that she would dine out for the rest of her life on the story of year 9 obediently getting on in near silence with maths work as instructed by their form captain in the absence of a teacher.

As a result of this more disciplined approach to their studies, in an independent school observed lesson you may well get through a great deal more material than you would normally expect, so be prepared with roughly twice the amount that you would usually have, in order not to run out. Organise it so that you can use all of it, or three-quarters, or half (i.e. what you actually would normally use), and the lesson would nonetheless still hang together as an overall unit.

You will also need a Plan B for the level of the lesson. Independent schools vary enormously, from those which have very high levels of attainment because they have academic selection, to others where the level would be more or less what you would expect from your own school. Look at their published examination results; how do these compare with a school to which you are accustomed? The high-flying schools may be two or even three years ahead; I saw this clearly when, as an experiment, I gave a year 9 pupil from another school the maths and English examination papers for year 7 entry at my independent school, papers that would be sat by year 6 pupils, three years younger. The year 9 failed to get a mark good enough to be admitted to my school in September for year 7, yet in his own school went that same September into year 10, then on to A-levels and university.

So try to gauge the level by looking online at their GCSE and A-level results for senior schools (the term secondary school is generally not used in the independent sector). For junior or preparatory schools, look at their SATs results (if they do them and publish them) or see which senior schools pupils move to at the end of their primary schooling. If it is prestigious and highly academic schools, they will have a good level.

This should give you an idea of the standard to expect in your lesson. Then decide whether you need to raise both the level of the work and your expectations of the pupils, with additional work both lower and higher available in case you have still got it wrong. The worst thing I see in observed lessons in independent schools is a lesson that is clearly of totally the wrong level, but the candidate sticks to the lesson plan like grim death.

Another surprise on occasion in an independent school is that at the end of the lesson the pupils may clap or thank you. Do not be too overwhelmed; it is the courteous thing for them to do to an outsider, and not what happens in normal lessons.

For independent schools, where of course the pay and contractual conditions of employment vary enormously, my advice is always to try to find out as much as possible about these before you apply, and certainly before you go to interview. It can be tricky to do this, especially if enquiring about maternity pay; your best bet is to e-mail the Business Manager or Bursar and ask. To try for anonymity, you may think that it would be best to do so from a completely different e-mail address, not the one that you use for your application, and one that does not include your name. But don't then include your name in the enquiry that you make in the body of the e-mail, as that would give the game away.

20. Video interview by Zoom, Facetime, Meet, Skype etc.

In normal times, pre-Covid, it was highly unlikely for you to be offered an interview with a school in England and Wales by Zoom, Facetime, Meet, Skype or similar technology, since the statutory guidance is that there should be a face-to-face interview. However, British schools abroad have often used this, as it is clearly much more cost effective, allowing them to interview a range of candidates who are far away.

During the Covid-19 pandemic, however, this became increasingly common in the UK too, and some schools have maintained it. Here is the advice for preparation of this type of interview.

You need to do your preparation for this just as much as for a face-to-face interview, with some extras to sort out. You should be aware that you need to trial the software several times if you are not already very familiar with it, and also need to think carefully about the visual impact that you will be making. So that's several things to be thinking about: what you say and how you say it, how you look on screen, and can you make the darned software work. On the plus side, unlike in a school-based interview, you can certainly wear your lucky SpongeBobSquarePants slippers.

For a video interview, there needs to be an appropriate background; it does not have to be a bookcase full of worthy tomes, but check out on screen that you don't have a standard lamp growing out of your head or part of an overflowing laundry basket in one corner.

But do not be tempted to produce a fancy virtual background, as that will just look like showing off your technology skills, will be distracting as they try to guess where it is, and will basically risk annoying the panel. A simple virtual background of a classroom would be OK, if your room is really ghastly. Make sure that you test it out well in advance. If your computer is not one of the newer models, you may need to hang pale green or cream material over obtrusive items in your real background that are showing through on the screen tests.

I would not have a blurred background, which is also an option on some software, as the panel members may be tempted to try and distinguish what it is that you are hiding, thus not concentrating on you.

My advice would be to keep it simple, don't stress over getting the right virtual background, I believe that videoing against a living-room wall with no virtual background, is fine.

You need to be well lit; it is said that the best is facing a large window, with natural light pouring in. Sunshine in your eyes making you squint is not good, however, and daylight may be impossible to have if the school is skyping you in the evening because they are on the other side of the world, in a different time zone. So you may need to draft in some extra lamps, as well as using the brightness settings on your app.

You usually need to have a laptop or tablet raised from its normal position, so that the camera is higher. Try putting a large dictionary – or even two - underneath it. Desktop PCs are usually at more or less the right height. I have the camera on my computers obscured by a small sticker in normal use, often only remembering to remove it when I see that there is no video for me during a Zoom or Meet. So that's the first place to investigate if your video seems to be not working. Next point is to check the video setting on screen – have you clicked something like *Join with video* for instance.

For clothes you need only worry about the top half; no need to get out the shoe polish. However, that top half fills all the screen, so needs to be perfect. You can go for something slightly less formal than in a face-to-face interview, but please keep it smart and refined. No beach tops, no vests, no cleavage.

Women do best to wear something plain in design, as a fussily patterned top will probably not look good, and can also sometimes make the screen go awry. Slipping shoulder straps will not impress either; a top with sleeves, sleeves of any length.

For men, a suit jacket is not necessary; a well-ironed shirt (the front half well ironed anyway!) with a tie, or a smart collared t-shirt, would be good. A t-shirt without a collar, or a sweatshirt, please don't. A wife-beater t-shirt is even less appropriate, but I guess that I don't need to tell you that. Keep the colours fairly sober too, and no green, not even a green tie, if you have a virtual background, as the background will bleed through to give an interesting effect.

Both sexes ensure that your hair is under control; flicking it out of your eyes will be even more distracting in close-up on screen than in real life.

You can have notes out of camera shot – best position is huge writing on sheets (wrapping paper?) just behind the screen, or postcard-sized notes stuck with tape on your computer above your screen so that they are visible right at eye level. Both of these are an improvement to peering down at a notepad by the side of your keyboard. Try with both, video yourself using them and see which comes over better.

Having organised your camera height, your clothes and your notes, do a trial recording of 5 minutes and see how you look. Then get a friend/partner/sibling to give you a video interview from another computer, so that they can give you feedback on how you appear. Some people in video interviews tend to lean towards the camera each time that they reply; this can look a bit weird, as though you are slightly tipsy. Get feedback too on what your expression is as you are listening to them; never forget that the camera is on you at all times. Look back at my earlier comments on your facial expression.

And smile, smile until your mouth wants to drop off your face. Smile as you are talking, as well as when you greet them. Not a big daft grin as though you are auditioning for the role of village idiot, but a small friendly smile all the time. It is especially important to look interested, and not bored or scared when they are speaking to you.

So having sorted all those technical bits out, then have somebody give you a mock interview (give them a list of possible questions to ask at random) using the actual technology (Zoom, etc), and record it, so that you can test how you look, how you sound, and if you make sense. And watch in particular how you react if they ask an unexpectedly tricky question.

Do also lock the door to prevent the children prancing into the room in the middle of the interview. Remember that poor BBC correspondent in South Korea?

If you share a flat or house, consider putting a notice on the door to remind your flatmates that – as you have already warned them fourteen times – between the hours of x and y, you're being interviewed for a job and you'd appreciate their being very quiet and not disturbing you. Promise wine and/or a take-away as a reward for their compliance.

Some international schools like also to hear from your non-teaching partner, to check that s/he knows what they are letting themselves in for and have plans not to get bored; warn him/her to be ready to step into camera view for a few minutes. Wearing appropriate clothing, of course, as if they, too, were on the interview spot.

Another innovation during the pandemic lockdown was that some schools are asking candidates to teach a lesson on-line during the interview. Yes, that's right. No pupils, so you teach it to the panel, pretending that they are KS1 pupils, or an A-level class.

A pretty daft idea in my view.

Now happily abandoned, but if in an interview for a school abroad you are unfortunate to have this, just play it straight, avoid the temptation to threaten detentions or no playtime, and have a superb lesson plan, including differentiation and possible follow-up work, to e-mail them beforehand.

21. A FEW OTHER QUESTIONS

PORTFOLIOS – YES OR NO?

There are a few occasions when you should take a portfolio. The first is if they specifically ask for one; this is more likely to be in primary, or if they are recruiting a NQT specifically. The second is if you are a NQT, and it makes you feel more confident. The third is if you are applying for a post in the visual arts: any art speciality, any design technology subject, and drama.

So what should be in these portfolios? For a general, i.e. not the art/dt/drama one, you should include some of these:

Schemes of work, lesson plans, examples of students' work coming out of those lessons

An extract from an exercise book to show the quality of your marking

Any teaching observations showing quality of teaching

Perhaps data on a teaching group and showing how you have differentiated to support the different ability groups

And if relevant, exam results, raw and value-added

If primary, photos of your classroom, including the displays

You may be concerned about including photos of pupils; check the school policy on photography. However, showing photos of pupils in a closed group in a school, with people who have all had DBS checks, could in no way be considered a risk or contrary to policy. Nonetheless, I suggest that you print off a copy of the school's photography policy and include it in the portfolio, to show that you are aware of this issue and the need to take care.

The visual arts portfolios should contain two separate sections: your own creative achievements and those of your pupils. You can go for a traditional hard copy portfolio, but I would consider using a website, with password protection or requiring the owner's agreement to view. A closed Facebook group even might be possible. You would tell the school about this in your application, and ask them to contact you to gain permission to view.

THE TRICKY QUESTION

T he tricky question may be being asked why you left a particular post, or why you wish to leave your current school. Normally it is not tricky at all, and you can refer back to the section *The best question to be asked at an interview* and see what I say about the question *What interests you about this post?* In fact, *Why do you wish to leave your current post?* is really the same question.

Do remember my comment on a school wanting pilgrims not refugees, so refer to your belief that you can contribute positively to this school, citing your USPs in one form or another. The emphasis should not be on why you are leaving one school, but on why you are enthusiastic about going to the other school and what you can offer it; what is their advantage, not yours. Do not mention your current school in your reply – remember the rule not to talk negatively?

The trickiness may come when you have left a full-time permanent post for less secure employment, lower-status employment, or none. There is a section in my previous book: *Applying for a Teaching Job 2022-3* on what reason to give for leaving a post, including in circumstances such as these. You may need to say, very briefly, that you felt that you could make a better and more valued contribution in another context. Keep it very brief, and however much they probe, give no examples of things done that you were uncomfortable with; a school would respect your discretion and loyalty.

The thing to remember is that you should always take care **not** to be negative about your current school at any moment. The prospective employer merely wants to know that you were not dismissed and that you did not quit on a whim, as either of those two could have consequences for their own school.

22. SENIOR LEADERSHIP INTERVIEWS

If you have just jumped straight to here from the table of contents, I suggest that you do not read only this section; the first part of the book has a great deal of information and advice that is relevant to you too. This section provides additional information, but not all the advice that you will need. If you read only this part, you will miss important points.

You may also wish to re-read my book on *Applying for a Teaching Job 2022-3*, in particular its section on SLT applications and the SLT advertisements calendar.

YOUR IMPACT AT THE INTERVIEW AS A PROSPECTIVE SCHOOL LEADER

T he overall impact that you make is one of the most important things during the selection process. If you have read the earlier sections first, you will have been reminded about the initial 30 or 60 or 120 second period when people make up their mind about you. A school leader must look, sound and act like a school leader. You must project the image of a leader in everything you say and do, and how you look, from the moment you step or drive onto the school premises. You must look calm and in control. You must have an aura of respect. You must look and act the part already.

I will add that you must not pick up litter, nor pick up coats left lying on the cloakroom floor.

By this I am saying that you must turn a blind eye to the things which you would note and immediately remedy in your own school. It is ingrained in us; I have to keep my hands firmly in my pockets in another school not to instinctively bend down to pick up litter, or to say to the nearest pupil: *"Could you just pick that up please and find a bin for it? Thank you"*. This would, of course, be discourteous in someone else's school, so ignore everything that you would normally deal with.

I cannot over-emphasise that the impact that you make is one of the keys to starting everything off positively. Your clothes, your overall personal presentation, your body language will all contribute to the impact that you make, and first impressions are lasting impressions, so make that first impression count. I have a colleague in the leadership recruitment business who asks reception who is wearing an anorak over their business suit. Or rather she asks them to confirm who was, as she claims to be able to identify anorak-wearers in the interview.

23. PREPARATION FOR THE SLT INTERVIEW

INFORMATION AVAILABLE

T he school – probably the clerk to the governors - will have sent out an information pack for candidates before the interview. Look through it and check that you have all the information that the school is willing to provide for candidates; beware the initiative test – could you ask for additional information which hasn't been included? How about their plans for the next 3 or 5 years? I was surprised, when applying for one headship, that the most recent set of management accounts – or indeed any accounts – was not included, and asked for both annual and management ones. I was told subsequently that nobody else had asked for any accounts at all. For independent schools, remember that you can get copies of past accounts on the Charities Commission website, to gain a picture over time.

You will need to do a good deal of research about the school; most of this will have been done before your application, and that may well have included a visit or the opportunity to speak to someone on the phone about the position. An opportunity to visit may also be offered at this stage, and you should do your very best to attend this. If you are fortunate, between the publication of the advertisement and the interview date, there is some type of open day for prospective pupils and parents at the school; do attend this, but in a low-key manner, do not introduce yourself.

The selection process will usually also include a school walk-round where you can get a feel for the school again; I say usually because occasionally for some headship appointments in the independent sector, a great deal of secrecy is involved. Candidates are interviewed on a schedule that ensures that no one candidate meets another, and they visit the school when it is closed, so that no member of staff sees and recognises them. This is to maintain candidate confidentiality in a fairly small world.

I would go well equipped to the interview, with a laptop, and hard copies of both a lesson observation template and your presentation summary, as well as all your application documents. Take also a memory stick with these documents on, and the presentation itself.

THE QUALITIES SOUGHT

I n the earlier, general, interview section I spoke about defining your USPs and identifying the school's BBs. That advice is all relevant here, so do make sure that you have read it carefully. I will add that for a school leadership post, there are BBs in addition to the ones in general that come out of their documentation and website. These are the essentials for your interviews, and indeed for life as a leader:

Vision

Leadership

Passion for the role

These must come out in your answers in the interview, and you will need to draft mind maps for each of these, with your understanding of what these represent for a school, and examples of how you have demonstrated these in your current post, and how you expect to demonstrate them in your new role.

MIND MAPPING

A s set out in the earlier section, mind mapping is the intelligent way to prepare. You will do mind maps based on the school's person specification, on its job description, on the ***Headteachers' Standards (2020)***, even if the post is AHT or DHT, as well as on your USPs and any other BBs you identify for the school. But you must also draft mind maps, and prepare thoroughly, on general leadership qualities and issues. A recent headship appointment process helpfully gave the candidates this list of areas that would be discussed in interview:

Raising attainment

Promoting inclusion

Staff development, management and finance

Pupils, parents and community

Your values in education

What is your vision for our School?

Together with the three general qualities defined earlier (vision, leadership, passion), this very helpful list should be the backbone of the mind maps for a leadership interview.

24. THE SLT SELECTION PROCESS

An interview for a SLT position can last just one day, with all the activities and the final interview taking place then, and the result announced that evening. This is the common pattern for primary schools, for deputy posts in secondaries, and some headships too. However the two-day interview, or on rare occasions, three, is also fairly common for headships, especially in the independent sector. The two days may not be consecutive but separated by a week or more, and not all candidates are taken forward to the final interview. The drawback of this, for a school, is that applicants may have other interviews, and receive job offers in the intervening period, so they lose some favoured candidates.

After day 1 of interviews for a headship, with 9 days to go before day 2, I received a phone call from the chair of governors. He enquired whether I had other interviews scheduled before their final interview; I had three in fact, as it was peak headship appointment period. He then asked me to withdraw from them all, as of the nine candidates in the first round, I was the only one being taken forward to the final stage. Why he could not have just made me the offer there and then, I shall never know; I had to wait nine days and do a presentation before I was appointed.

Different people may be involved in day 1 and day 2, with more governors in at the final stage. Occasionally day 1 is not managed by the school at all, but by the leadership recruitment agency, who may interview a dozen or more candidates, on their premises, over a couple of days, and then pass to the school their comments on each one for the shortlisting to be done.

Who, in fact, is likely to be on the interview panel? For a deputy or assistant head position, then the headteacher will be there; the deputy will be there too, unless it is his/her post that is being filled. It is considered good practice in appointments that the outgoing colleague is not involved in any way in the appointment of the replacement. I have, however, seen this breached in appointments in both FE colleges and independent schools, where the prospective principals and headteachers were interviewed, individually, by the outgoing post-holder. The reasoning behind this bar is to ensure that the new appointment is open to all; with the current person involved, there might be a tendency to repeat the previous appointment, and select somebody similar in views and outlooks, rather than having a wider choice.

There will be at least three governors for headships in maintained schools, perhaps just one or two for DHT and AHT, with the chair of governors normally chairing the interview panel. *The School Staffing (England) Regulations 2009 (as amended 2012)*, which apply to maintained schools, set out the process for appointing headteachers. N.B. the document *Staffing and employment advice for schools, October 2021*, is an addition to this, very useful, and I recommend it for anyone on or aspiring to SLT as general development.

Regulation 15 of the 2009 regulations states that when recruiting a headteacher, the governing body must appoint a selection panel which consists of at least three governors, other than a governor who is the head teacher or (as the case may be) a deputy head teacher. Academies, free schools and independent schools do not have to abide by this.

If the school is part of a trust or group, there will be representatives from these. In such cases, the CEO of the trust, as the senior person present, is most likely to chair the panel, and is probably the person whose views will carry most weight. There may also be an external consultant, such as myself, a representative from the local authority, from the diocese, or from the leadership recruitment agency.

ACTIVITIES FOR SLT SELECTION DAYS

There is no set pattern for either what sort of activity you have to do, nor for which activities are on which day, except that the full-blown final interview is at the end. The main thing to remember is that all the activities are designed to be do-able; there is no point in having tasks which are almost impossible and eliminate most candidates. Here are some possible schedules and possible activities.

Day 1 – normally at the school for 6-8 candidates. There may have been an initial weeding-out by consultants or leadership recruitment agency from a long list of 12-15.

A wide range of activities, in carousel format

Short listing at the end

A new task given to candidates for day 2. If that is the next day, it means homework that night, usually a presentation

Day 2 – normally but not always in the school. 3-4 candidates

Presentation or other task – sometimes unseen and given on the day with very short preparation time

Final interview

GENERAL OVERVIEW OF THE DIFFERENT ACTIVITIES IN A SLT INTERVIEW

At some time during the two days, you will almost certainly have some or most of the following activities; which and how many depending on the post (AHT, DHT, HT).

A presentation to the interview panel

A presentation to some staff

A student panel interview

Carousel of short interactions with small staff groups on different topics

A data analysis exercise

An in-tray exercise

A planning activity

A finance task

A lesson observation with feedback

Teach a lesson (primary only – very unlikely in secondary)

An assembly

For independent schools, there may be a marketing task

You will doubtless be relieved to hear that you are not going to have to do all of that – it wouldn't fit into two days – and that what used to be a popular activity in days gone by has been largely abandoned. This is the so-called "Goldfish bowl" when the candidates are all pitted against each other in a free-for-all role-play called *the round-table observed activity*. It was horrendous to be in, and horrendous to try and observe and come to any sensible conclusions.

Most of those activities you probably deal with in your current post, although some less often than others. For posts other than HT you may have less direct experience. I suggest that for these less experience areas (which may be whole-school data analysis, finance or strategic planning), you speak to the person who leads on these issues in your school, and ask for a little tuition. It would not be reasonable to expect a candidate to have strengths in all areas, so do not be over-concerned if you feel that you don't perform as well as you would have hoped in some of them.

IN-TRAY EXERCISES

These come in and out of fashion; you may have come across them when being appointed to your current post, or indeed have used them yourself for appointing new colleagues. The basic rule here is not to be overwhelmed; often it is not expected that candidates will manage to complete the task in the timescale, merely to see how they cope under pressure and if they can prioritise correctly; if you cannot write notes on everything, then the least important issues should be the ones unfinished. Therefore, the urgent and important issues come first. Could it be put aside for half an hour without any loss of efficiency or safety? Year 9 left on their own perhaps could not, for example.

Do remember that there may be a school policy on some things. You cannot be expected to know their policies, but can at least mention that you would check the school policy and procedures.

Here are some examples of the type of issue that you might be faced with in an exercise of this kind, or, indeed, when working in a school or college. N.B. these are examples culled from various sets of exercises; you would not be expected to tackle a list this long in half an hour. I would expect half a dozen items. These examples are a mixture of secondary and primary, and relate to different levels of responsibility in the leadership team. It would be useful for you, as you read them, to mentally classify each one as urgent, important or neither, can be delegated or not, need to consult policies, etc.

One of your responsibilities is that of arranging cover for colleagues who are on courses. A head of department comes to your office. She explains that because year 11 are on study leave and year 10 are on a cross-curricular day, all four members of the department are teaching for only two out of the nine periods next Tuesday. She wants to devote the whole day to internal modernisation of students' GCSE course work, thereby needing cover from colleagues in other departments.

As the students were coming into school this morning, you noticed that something was going on between three girls in year 8. Katie and Nicola, both of whom have something of a reputation for aggressive behaviour, appeared to be bullying Chelsea, a much quieter girl. When you intervened, Chelsea insisted that 'we were just mucking around', but you were not convinced.

Mr Johnson announced to his Year 10 Maths class yesterday that there would be a class detention next week because their behaviour had been so bad. Two very well behaved and well-motivated students come to tell you that they are unhappy about it. 'It's not our fault. Mr Johnson can't control some of the class, and we all get the blame'.

Mrs Ballinger has written to you voicing concern about a trip that has been offered to her daughter Grace (Year 10). You know nothing about this as it is not on the list of approved school visits, but apparently, Mrs Green, the teacher of GCSE Textiles, has suggested that some of the girls would benefit from looking at how fabrics are used in fashion. She is therefore taking six of them to look at fashion boutiques in a local shopping mall instead of their P.E. lessons; this is half an hour away on the bus. Mrs Long has told the parents in a letter that the girls will travel together to the mall at lunchtime on Wednesday and make their own way directly home at the end of the afternoon. Mrs Ballinger is worried that there is not enough supervision.

You receive a telephone call from the local police asking you to provide parents' names and addresses of two boys in year 9 and 10 (known to you as less than angels) who may be able to help them in an enquiry about underage drinking.

An aggrieved teacher comes and complains that she goes to Assembly every day, but others do not. She hands you a spreadsheet logging poor Assembly attendance of three colleagues over the past two terms.

At 11.30 am you are travelling back from a meeting at another school when you call into a supermarket 10 miles from school; you notice in the store a colleague who telephoned in ill that morning.

The headteacher has been teaching Year 7 French this year; MFL is part of the curriculum area that you manage as assistant headteacher. An anonymous letter is sent to you purporting to come from a group of parents, and complaining that he just gets the students to sit working through exercises while he sits at the computer apparently answering his e-mails.

You have just written your first letter to parents as the new deputy headteacher. We have run off 850 copies and when you ask one of the office staff to place them in registers she points out that there is a spelling error.

A parent phones you concerned that her son in year 11, who has been predicted an A* in English, has received a B grade for the last two pieces of coursework since being taught by a new member of staff.

The headteacher is away from the school and you have executive powers. At 8.40 am, you have a telephone call from a sixth-form student saying that a Year 7 girl has been knocked down on the nearby major road and seems to be seriously injured.

You receive the following note from the head of PE. 'I am

worried about Susan Watkins in my PE group. I noticed some major bruises on her arms and torso while she was changing today. She knows I saw but I didn't like to say anything. Please advise me'.

A head of department comes to see you to complain that a member of staff is constantly late to lessons and also failing to turn up for her lunchtime duty.

Your secretary tells you that while you were in assembly, the local paper rang about a rumour that a member of staff hit a child yesterday in a maths class.

The school nurse tells you that a teacher to whom she handed out two paracetamol this morning was smelling strongly of alcohol.

Three sets of parents have written in to say that they are going on holiday two days before the end of term, as the airfares are cheaper. How will this be entered on the registers?

Draft a response to a parent requesting a day off in term time for a pupil to see a television celebrity open the local supermarket.

You are just about to go into assembly that you are due to lead when a parent turns up demanding to speak to you immediately and threatening to take his complaint to the local paper.

Today's Daily Telegraph has a photo of the crowd at Wimbledon. Clearly visible are the Year 1 Teaching Assistant and her daughter, a pupil in year 6, who were both away ill yesterday with gastric flu.

After school, you pop into the year 5 classroom and find the teacher's son, a 14-year-old at a different school, surfing the MIS records (password-protected access) and noting down details of staff home addresses.

Your secretary hands you, in silence, screen grabs from the

Facebook page of a teacher with negative comments about the senior leadership team.

Help! 5 pregnant teachers out of a total of 13! And all of them have asked for a half-time jobshare when they return.

From the enclosed SATs results, write five bullet points for a presentation to governors.

Write two reasons for and two reasons against KS2 SATs

Mrs Brown has phoned to say that today, she and five other mothers are coming in to eat school dinners, as they are not convinced that they are healthy or worth the money.

THE CAROUSEL
OF ACTIVITIES

T he carousel can include any of the activities suggested in the general list above, or it can be a carousel of three or four interviews with small groups concentrating on one aspect of the role. However, it can sometimes be more challenging, as the example below from a large academy shows. In this, the candidates meet six different panels for 15-20 minutes, beginning each panel meeting with a 3-4 minute presentation. They are given half an hour at the beginning of the day to write out brief notes in preparation for all six of these.

This is clearly requiring quick thinking and a solid knowledge of the many issues that could face the academy. If you are faced with this marathon (I hope that you will not), then try also to identify the likely main BB of each panel. Here are the details:

Selection of new Principal: range of leadership styles, skills and experiences

This half-day session will be devoted to a carousel of panel discussions on specified topics. Each discussion will be with a different panel, and you will have a choice of topics for each one. This will enable us to explore with you your range of leadership styles, skills and experiences.

As each discussion lasts only 15 - 20 minutes, there will be no time for the panel to present themselves individually; you will identify yourself on entering and then give a brief (3-4 minutes) presentation of your views on the topic selected. This will be followed by questions and discussion. You will note that the panel may also wish to question you on the topic(s) that you chose not to present, and indeed on any other relevant area of interest.

For each topic selected, you should be prepared to speak on the following three aspects:

* The challenges or issues as you identify them

* How you would deal with these in the context of our Academy

* One specific example of your personal experience of the same/ similar issue

You may now read the topics and select those that you will discuss. You have 30 minutes to prepare your brief notes.

Common panel interviews – selection of topics

All candidates will meet the following 5 panels; you should select ONE topic only for each.

Panel A: Vision

Developing vision, OR

Implementing vision

Panel B: Governance

Working with Governors, OR

Working with sponsors

Panel C: Finance

Managing budget £9M, OR

Accessing alternative sources of funding

Panel D: HR

TUPE, OR

Capability, OR

Disciplinary

Panel E: Curriculum

Raising D/E to C, OR

Appropriate vocational qualifications for our Academy

Additional panel interview – selection of topics

Candidates will be allocated at random to one of the panels below; you should select ONE topic only for each.

Panel F: Communities

Travellers, OR

Refugees, OR

Illegal immigrants

Panel G: Pastoral

Gang culture, OR

White working-class males, OR

Forced marriages

Panel H: Legal

Health & Safety, OR

Equality Act 2010, OR

Safeguarding

THE STUDENT COUNCIL

S tudent council Interviews are generally tightly controlled by the school, to ensure that the same questions go to each candidate and that the procedure is therefore fair. It also protects the school's reputation by avoiding troublesome student members and embarrassing questions. You will need to think what are the BBs of this group; they will be different from those of the interview panel. I quote below some interesting comments made by students at secondary level, on being interviewed by a leadership recruitment consultant when their school was seeking a new headteacher. These are the sort of views to consider.

Kind, but can be strict at times

Committed, wants to improve the school

Takes time to know the students on a personal level

Communicates in a positive way

Open minded, fun

Willing to listen to pupils' and teachers' ideas and take them on board

Believes all students are worth the effort

Supports extra-curricular activities

Up-to-date and has time for students

Welcomes students from different backgrounds

A good classroom teacher

Approachable, not scary

Cares about every student

Someone prepared to make long-term change and stay here long enough to see it through

THE PRESENTATION

When there is a two-day selection process, the presentation is almost always on the second day, although sometimes you are asked to do one on day 1, then a different one on day 2. The topic could be just about anything related to the vision and leadership of a school. Even if those two key words are not in the title, do ensure that you drop them into your presentation. Remember your audience; governors are not always up to date with all the acronyms that we use, so do not bandy them about. Here are a few possible topics:

My major career success

Raising achievement in my current school

The future of the primary curriculum

How I lead staff through the GCSE changes

My vision for Grungy Green School in 5 years' time

Primary assessment – how I reduce its negative impact on staff and pupils

The general interview section earlier had some advice on presentations. You should be fairly well accustomed to giving presentations at this stage of your career, and know all the Do's and Don'ts. It is probably still worth while reminding yourself of the major ones, so do spend ten minutes refreshing your memory about no over-reliance on flashy technology, speaking from the heart not from a script, well-structured three-part presentation (introduction, main thesis, conclusion), eye contact, good pacing with appropriate pauses, good timing (with Plan B to know what to leave out or even add if timing going wrong), thank them at the end. Effective communication is an important feature of all school leadership, so you need to get this just right.

WHY YOU WERE ASKED NOT TO COME TO THE SECOND STAGE INTERVIEW

A discussion with a colleague also involved in leadership appointments came up with the following concerns about candidates aspiring to SLT posts; these are often the main justifications for a candidate not progressing to stage 2 of the interview.

An efficient and effective manager, but little sign of leadership

Insufficient positive experience to step up to the next level

Little evidence of a whole-school approach in examples given, seems still to be thinking in terms of just his/her faculty

Does not understand the complexities of the role

Or does understand them and is slightly alarmed by that

Too democratic; could s/he have that difficult conversation and take the tough decisions?

Their school is performing well, but how much of that is down to them, to what extent are they merely being carried on the crest of someone else's wave?

25. THE AFTERMATH

After your interview you will need to do a careful analysis of the questions that you were asked, the answers that you gave, the tasks that you carried out, and how you believe that you fared; this will form part of the planning for the next interview, if you were not successful this time. I suggest that you start this as soon as possible, in public transport on the way home even.

The earlier section on interviews in general gave you all the advice that you need on the period after the interview, including on how to accept the job offer once, hopefully, you are successful and receive that eagerly-awaited phone call. Do go back and re-read that so you are fully prepared for that big moment. You will need also to be sure about how to respond in writing to the offer, so that your first contacts with the school after getting the job are very professional.

I would like to wish you all the very best in your interview, and trust that this book has been helpful.

If you have found this book to be useful, please do give it a brief review on

its Amazon page. Thank you.

If you have spotted typos or other errors, please send me a Direct Message via Twitter @Theo_Griff – my account is open to receive DMs.

Best wishes for your interview for a job in teaching.

Printed in Great Britain
by Amazon

21756471R00106